The Complete Guide to

CABINETS & COUNTERTOPS

How to Customize Your Home with Cabinetry

COOL
SPRINGS
PRESS
Home and Garden Experts™

MINNEAPOLIS, MINNESOTA

First published in 2013 by Cool Springs Press, an imprint of the Quayside Publishing Group, 400 First Avenue North, Suite 400, Minneapolis, MN 55401

The information in this book is true and complete to the best of our knowledge. All recommendations are made without any guarantee on the part of the author or Publisher, who also disclaims any liability incurred in connection with the use of this data or specific details.

Cool Springs Press titles are also available at discounts in bulk quantity for industrial or sales-promotional use. For details write to Special Sales Manager at Cool Springs Press, 400 North First Avenue, Suite 400, Minneapolis, MN 55401 USA. To find out more about our books, visit us online at www.coolspringspress.com.

Acquisitions Editor: Mark Johanson
Design Manager: Brad Springer
Layout: Laurie Young
Edition Editor: Chris Peterson
Contributing Editor: Chris Marshall

Library of Congress Cataloging-in-Publication Data

The complete guide to cabinets & countertops : how to customize your home with cabinetry.
    pages cm
  At head of title: Black & Decker
  Includes index.
  ISBN 978-1-59186-589-6 (softcover)
  1. Cabinetwork--Amateurs' manuals. 2. Countertops--Amateurs' manuals. I. Title: Complete guide to cabinets and countertops. II. Title: Black & Decker.

  TT197.C656 2013
  684.1'6--dc23

                                    2013009478

Printed in China
10 9 8 7 6 5 4 3 2 1

The Complete Guide to Cabinets & Countertops
Created by: The Editors of Creative Publishing international, Inc., in cooperation with Black & Decker.
Black & Decker® is a trademark of The Black & Decker Corporation and is used under license.

NOTICE TO READERS

For safety, use caution, care, and good judgment when following the procedures described in this book. The publisher and Black & Decker cannot assume responsibility for any damage to property or injury to persons as a result of misuse of the information provided.

The techniques shown in this book are general techniques for various applications. In some instances, additional techniques not shown in this book may be required. Always follow manufacturers' instructions included with products, since deviating from the directions may void warranties. The projects in this book vary widely as to skill levels required: some may not be appropriate for all do-it-yourselfers, and some may require professional help.

Consult your local building department for information on building permits, codes, and other laws as they apply to your project.

Contents

The Complete Guide to
Cabinets & Countertops

Contents (Cont.)

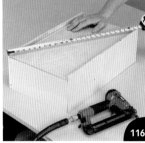

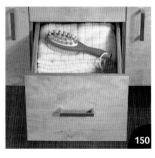

Introduction

Few home improvements can transform the look and function of a room more dramatically than new cabinets and countertops. Install a set of cabinets in a laundry room, and suddenly the space is not only more handsome, it's actually a more pleasant and efficient place for washing clothes. Another popular improvement, new kitchen countertops, can completely revitalize the appearance of the room while improving storage and adding durable work surfaces. Even areas that you don't normally think of as cabinetry rooms, like bedrooms and mudrooms, can reap enormous benefits from a few strategically placed cabinets.

As useful and as beautiful as they can be, however, even modest cabinets and countertops represent a significant investment in time, money, and effort. You'll want to choose carefully so that you install permanent home furnishings that meet your storage and work-surface needs perfectly, while fitting in with your décor for a long time to come.

The truth is, appearance and function are inextricably intertwined in these high-impact home elements. Some countertops are tough enough to withstand hot pots, fend off knife cuts, and resist stains: quite possibly your primary objective. Others are fabulously attractive, but a little less tough. On the cabinetry side, you can choose a traditional face-frame cabinet style that practically assures you'll have no design failures, but at the expense of maximizing your storage space and perhaps doing something a little more creative.

The bottom line, when it comes to cabinets and countertops, is that your cabinet and countertop decisions must strike a balance between function and form. Fortunately, you will find no lack of choices when you visit your local building center or specialty supplier, and all of them can be put to work to help you with that balance.

Countertops can be created with a vast array of materials, from the simplest post-form prefabs to imported marble or granite tile. There is also an increasing number of countertop choices that are both beautiful and eco-friendly, including recycled paper and recycled glass versions. This wealth of choices also has meant that there are more inexpensive options available than ever before—as well as more high-tech and high-end choices.

You'll face a similar range of options when choosing cabinets as you will when choosing countertops. Although there are really two basic types—face-frame and frameless—there are countless options within those two divisions. Door styles themselves vary from simple flat "slab" panels to incredibly ornate, handcrafted rail-and-stile versions, and then to even less traditional options like glass fronts, which themselves come in a range of styles. You can choose the convenience of stock cabinets, semi-custom, or entirely custom-made. And your options don't stop there. You'll find many specialty features like pull-out spice racks and extendable cutting boards that can make your cabinets even more useful.

Whether you're building and installing cabinets and countertops yourself, having someone install them, or something in between, you'll find all the information you need in the pages that follow. We've included insight to help you make the decision in the first place, and projects that will teach you all the skills and techniques you'll need to tackle any countertop or cabinet installation.

Gallery of Countertops

Go stunning on a budget with a new laminate countertop. The looks available in modern laminate are incredibly varied … and incredibly realistic. The faux stone countertop shown here is a prime example of what can be achieved with the latest laminate products and a tight budget.

Pick from a variety of edge profiles with laminates. Long gone are the basic flat drop fronts of your mother's laminate countertops; modern versions offer a wealth of edge profiles. The choices include the rounded look shown here, which effectively carries through the illusion of a real stone surface. You can also opt for thicker drop fronts, highly detailed profiles, and many more.

Today's laminates deliver texture too! A mica-flecked engineered surface? Hardly. This is a laminate countertop with a top texture that re-creates all the imperfections of the most intriguing stone surface. Combined with the amazingly realistic appearance, laminate textures add a whole new dimension of options for any homeowner looking for a low-cost, stunning countertop.

Genuine quartz can be a stunning alternative to marble or granite. This "green" material is mined using eco-friendly methods, is incredibly durable, and simply looks luxurious. This white surface, with its bump-out sink edge, is clear evidence of the marvelous looks that can be achieved with quartz.

Add a splash of scintillating pattern to any kitchen with a quartz countertop. The mesmerizing, flowing design in this stone surface contrasts the solid-colored surfaces throughout the space and creates a high-quality focal point in the room.

Turn to unusual materials for a stunning look in a hallmark room. This mirrored bathroom is perfectly accented by a scintillating blue countertop formed of polished volcanic rock. Durable, waterproof, and available in a painter's palette of colors, these countertops are ideal in wet spaces where you want to make a design statement.

Add a magical color element to your kitchen with a volcanic rock countertop. The manufacturing process used to create these surfaces allows for colors from bold to nuanced, creating unique appearances that are truly one-of-kind. The counters in this room combine an intriguing visual depth with an incredibly hard, durable material.

Gallery of Countertops

Choose a recycled glass countertop for an enduring surface that sparkles under natural or artificial light. This subtle version fits right in with the sophisticated cabinets, backsplash, and accessories in this kitchen, but small variations in the color of the glass used create small, lovely focal points throughout the countertop. Even when it's time to update the kitchen, the countertop can remain as a timeless part of the design.

Spruce up an otherwise sedate kitchen design with an island countertop of recycled glass. Not only is this counter a wonderful departure from the neutral, solid-colored surfaces throughout the space, it's also incredibly durable—making a wonderful work surface.

Take advantage of the fun color potential recycled glass countertops offer. This upbeat, whimsical, and colorful kitchen is perfectly accented with a recycled glass countertop featuring a rainbow of colors that looks like parade confetti. This particular countertop was a brilliant choice, one that holds its own in a bright and bold kitchen design.

Create a sophisticated look in the kitchen with granite countertops. Incredibly hard, heat-resistant and available in a range of colors and patterns, this stone is a luxury choice. But it doesn't have to break the bank; the countertops shown here are actually thinner than normal with drop fronts that make it appear as if they are solid granite. It's an eco-friendly option because it makes use of granite scraps, not to mention saving the homeowner money.

Go eco-friendly in your kitchen by using a sustainable wood countertop. The bamboo used to make this lovely countertop-and-backsplash combo is fast-growing and can be fabricated to create a number of appearances from the blonde strips here, to much more exotic colors and grain patterns.

Mix incredible durability with a unique appearance by choosing a solid-surface countertop. A countertop like the Corian® units shown here are colored through and through so that you don't have to worry about scratches. And the colors and patterns available are enough to boggle the mind.

Gallery of Countertops

Opt for illusion if you want to save money, help the environment, and still have a super handsome countertop. This recycled paper countertop looks like slate and weighs every bit as much. It is water resistant, and is easy to install and maintain. The material can be cut to different shapes, and comes in a wide range of appearances and colors.

Use countertops to balance the rest of the room's design. Here, pure white recycled paper countertops are ideal to counteract the effect of dark cabinets in a small kitchen. The surfaces also moderate the busy patterns in the space and perfectly match the farmhouse apron sink. These paper countertops can be finished semi-gloss or polished to a high-gloss, making them even more adaptable across a variety of kitchen décor styles.

Leather? No, paper. Recycled paper countertops allow you to choose a convincingly faux leather or stone countertop that is much easier to install and usually lower cost. These counters can also be fabricated with many different edge profiles, adding even more variety to the look.

Gallery of Cabinets

Choose face-frame cabinetry for a traditional look that is timeless and classic. The elegant brown finish of these detailed cabinets is as practical as it is beautiful, because it won't show small smudges and stains as a lighter color might. The finish also matches the door and island table extension, and complements the wood floor.

Frameless cabinets don't have to equal cold, spare appearances. These stunning cherry-finish frameless cabinets are warm and stylish, and perfectly accent the other fixtures and appliances in the room. All for a less than what similar framed cabinets would have cost.

Gallery of Cabinets

Add eye-catching and practical function to any bathroom with a full-height set of cabinets like this country-style unit. Equipped with special pull-out racks, the cabinets become even more useful and well suited to particular toiletries and linens that should be stored in the room.

Make your kitchen a showplace with custom cabinetry in stunning high style. Glass fronts are an elegant addition to any kitchen, but glass fronts with one-of-a-kind details like the curving elements shown here—and replicated in the kitchen's windows— are a stylistic flourish that elevates the look of the kitchen.

Accessorize your kitchen to meet your cooking needs. Today's cabinetry includes a wealth of specialized features that you can include to make cooking and food preparation easy and pleasurable. This spice rack is one of a vast number of cabinetry options aimed at the avid home cook.

Spruce up a laundry while adding a lot of useful storage space with a few simple cabinets. These frameless units add a handsome look to the laundry room and plentiful storage for detergents and clothes. Frameless cabinets are a good choice for the laundry room because they maximize interior storage areas and allow for ease of access.

Create abundant extra storage by adding cabinets to almost any room in the house. This window seat structure makes the most of display shelves built on top of a low-slung cabinet unit that is useful and attractive. The shelves have been built and painted to match the detailing and finish of the cabinet unit, which creates a lovely unified overall appearance.

Tailor your cabinet choices to your storage needs. This inviting window seat includes a cabinet bench with a simple, deep drawer that is ideal for storing blankets and other bed linens that are used on a seasonal basis.

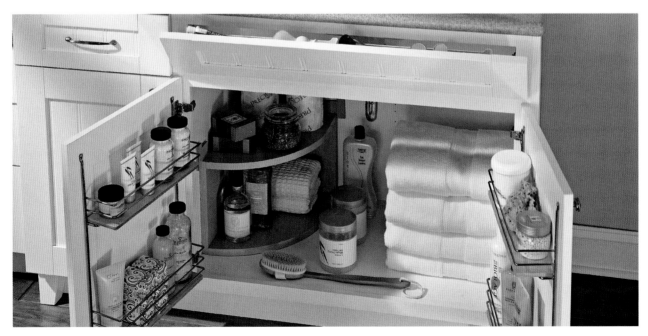

Create a spa-like experience by organizing bathroom luxury toiletries in a customized vanity cabinet. The tilt-out makeup drawer, wire door-mount shelves, and corner shelves all combine to make this vanity cabinet significantly more useful than it would be if left plain.

Tools & Materials

Installing cabinets and countertops is all about precision. Getting it right means using the correct tools, but it also means using tools that are in good shape—like saw blades that are sharp enough to ensure against chipping. As a bonus, having exactly the tools you need, when you need them, will make detailed installation processes go much quicker and easier. Last but certainly not least, with the help of the right tools in the right condition, you'll wind up with cabinets and countertops that look sharp for years, if not decades, to come.

The good news is that many of the tools you'll need for any cabinet or countertop project are probably in your toolbox right now. The better news is, the tools you might need buy—a router or biscuit joiner, for instance—will be incredibly useful for other woodworking and general DIY projects around the house. Unlike some plumbing or specialty project tools, the implements you'll need to install any cabinet or countertop are useful for many different applications.

The tools you'll need for most cabinet and countertop installations can be broken down into two basic groups: measuring and marking tools, and fabrication and installation tools.

MEASURING & MARKING TOOLS

Measuring and marking tools help you prepare cabinet and countertop materials for fabrication, set up the location for proper installation, and are your first line of defense against small inaccuracies that will lead to glaring errors in the finished product. Errors are difficult and expensive to fix, so these tools are vitally important. Fortunately, most measuring and marking tools are reasonably inexpensive and provide easy ways of measuring for level, square, and plumb. Technologies have advanced even among these simple tools, and you'll find levels, stud finders, and tape measures with built-in lasers, making them more accurate than ever before (though at a slightly higher price).

- A tape measure is one of the most common tools, and the odds are good that you already own at least one. (Keep one in the car for trips to the home center or lumberyard.) For cabinetry and countertop projects, you'll need a 25-ft. tape measure. It has a wider and thicker reading surface than a 16-ft. variety, making any measuring job a whole lot easier. If you can't tell the difference between the smaller lines on

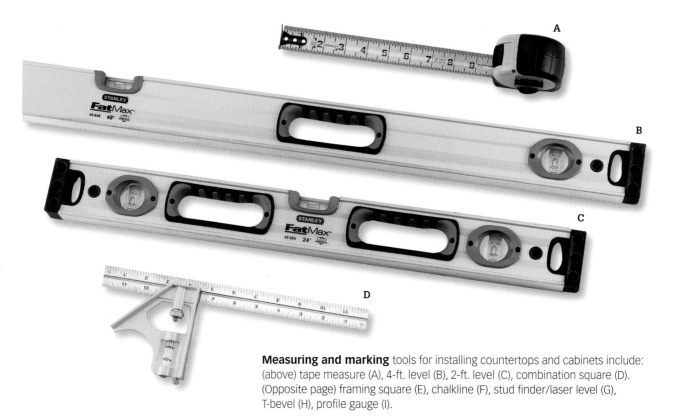

Measuring and marking tools for installing countertops and cabinets include: (above) tape measure (A), 4-ft. level (B), 2-ft. level (C), combination square (D). (Opposite page) framing square (E), chalkline (F), stud finder/laser level (G), T-bevel (H), profile gauge (I).

a standard tape, consider purchasing an "easy read" variety. It's essential that you read the tape accurately because this is where a lot of mistaken countertop cuts start.

- A framing square, also known as a carpenter's square, is commonly used to mark surfaces for cutting and to check for square. This is especially important for cutting countertop sections that will be joined with a butt joint.

- Chalk lines are used to make temporary straight lines anywhere one is needed. The case of a chalk line, or the "box," is teardrop-shaped so that the tool can double as a plumb bob. Use a chalk line to mark walls for ledger or cabinet placement, and countertops for cutting. Just keep in mind that chalk can be difficult to remove from porous surfaces like unsealed stone countertops.

- A stud finder is used to locate the framing members in a wall or ceiling. Higher-priced versions also locate plumbing, electrical, or other mechanicals inside the wall. Although stud finders are not completely necessary, they're a big convenience when hanging a large kitchen's worth of cabinets.

- Levels are available in a variety of lengths and price ranges. The longer the level, the higher the price. The two most commonly used sizes are 2-ft. and 4-ft. lengths. A 2-ft. level is handy for tight spaces, while the 4-ft. variety serves as a better all-purpose level. Laser levels are handy for creating a level line around the perimeter of a room or for establishing level lines over longer lengths. They provide a wide range of line or spot placement, depending on the model.

- A T-bevel is a specialized tool for finding and transferring angles precisely. T-bevels are generally used in conjunction with a power miter saw to find the angle of nonsquare corners. This tool is especially handy in older homes where the original states of square, plumb, and level may no longer apply.

- A profile gauge uses a series of pins to re-create the profile of any object so that you can transfer it to a work piece. These are essential when running a profiled backsplash into a perpendicular profiled backsplash section. Profile gauges are especially useful when scribing to an irregular wall.

- A combination square is a multifunction tool that provides an easy reference for 45- and 90-degree angles, as well as marking reveal lines or a constant specific distance from the edge of a work piece.

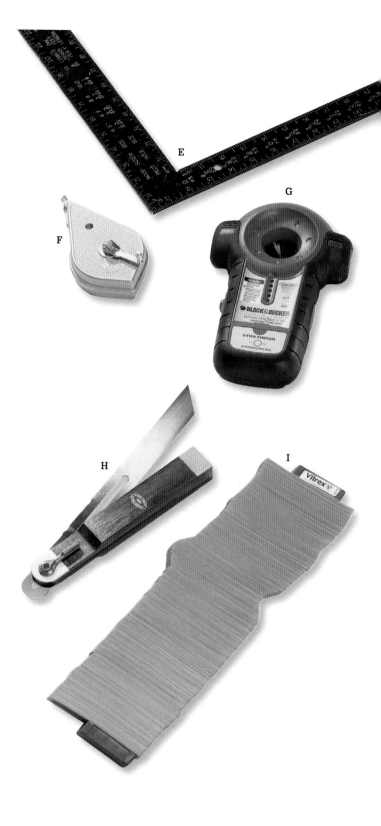

INSTALLATION & FABRICATION TOOLS

- A good quality hammer is a must for every cabinetry project. A curved claw hammer, otherwise known as a finish hammer, is a good all-purpose choice. Some people prefer a larger straight claw hammer for heavy tear-down projects and rough framing, but these hammers are too clumsy and heavy for driving smaller casing and finish nails, and tend to mar the surface of trim.

- Utility knives are available with fixed, folding, or retractable blades. As the name indicates, the tool is useful for an amazing variety of tasks from cutting drywall to back-beveling miter joints. Keep additional blades on hand (most knives have storage in the handle). Folding fixed-blade versions offer the durability and strength of a fixed blade with the protection of a folding handle.

- A set of chisels can be a big plus when installing cabinet door hardware as well as notching trim around obstacles and final fitting of difficult pieces.

- A coping saw has a thin, flexible blade designed to cut curves, and is used for making professional trim joints on inside corners. Coping saw blades should be fine toothed, between 16 and 24 teeth per inch for most hardwoods.

- A sharp handsaw is convenient for quick cut-offs and in some instances where power saws are difficult to control. Choose a crosscut saw meant for general-purpose cutting.

- Protective wear, including safety glasses and ear protection, is key any time you are working with loud tools or those that kick up fragments or dust. Dust masks are necessary when sanding, doing demolition, or when working around fumes.

- Pry bars come in a variety of sizes and shapes. A quality forged high-carbon steel flat bar is one of the most useful. They make quick work of existing cabinets when you need to demo a space prior to updating cabinets and countertops. No matter what type of pry bar you use, protect finished surfaces such as floors with a block of wood when using the bar.

- Side cutters and end nippers are useful for cutting off and pulling out bent nails. The added handle length and curved head of end nippers makes them ideal for pulling larger casing nails. Pneumatic brad nails and smaller pins will pull out easier with side cutters. Purchase a nail set for countersinking nail heads. Three-piece sets are available for different nail sizes.

- A rasp and metal file set are used to fit joints precisely and take the edges off of certain types of counters. The variety of shapes, sizes, and mills allow for faster rough removal of material, or smoother slow removal, depending on which you choose.

- Use a putty knife to fill nail holes with wood filler and for light scraping tasks.

- Clamps are crucial for holding cabinets and countertops correctly in position when fitting sections together, as well as for other chores.

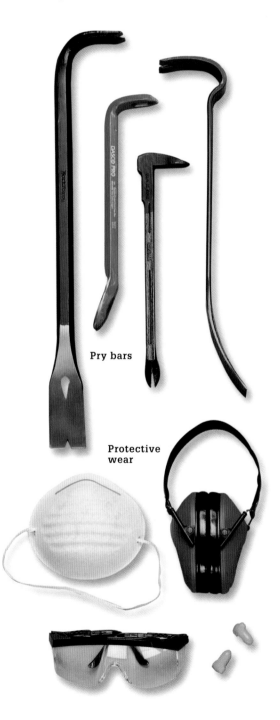

Pry bars

Protective wear

Handsaws

Putty knife

Nail sets

Hammer

Utility knives

Coping saw

Rasp and metal file set

Side cutters and end nippers

Block plane

Chisels

Power Tools

The right power tools can make fabricating and installing countertops and cabinets much easier and quicker. Different cabinet or countertop materials may require different tools, but the ones shown here represent a well-rounded collection that gives you a weapon for any task you face. Some, such as a power miter box, are crucial for truly professional results. Look to buy power tools that you'll use on a regular basis even after your cabinets and countertops are installed. Buy quality and the extra cost will be amortized in the long run. When the job calls for a more specialized power tool, it's usually wisest to rent it.

- A cordless drill (and bit set) is a must-have around the house, and especially for cabinetry work. Add a **hole saw** and a **pocket jig** to the mix and you're set to work with cabinets and countertops of every type.
- A circular saw is ideal for straight cuts and quick cut-offs of solid material. Carbide-tipped blades are recommended for most countertop surfaces, while a general-purpose blade will work for rough-cutting chores.
- A jigsaw is the perfect tool for cutting curves or sink cutouts in solid-surface countertops. Jigsaw blades come in an array of designs for different

Compound power miter saw

Circular saw

Jigsaw

Reciprocating saw

Cordless drill and bits

Router

Random orbit sander

Biscuit joiner

Power planer

Finish sander

Belt sander

Table saw

styles of cuts and different types and thicknesses of materials. Always use the right type of blade and do not force the saw during the cut or it may bend or break.

- A biscuit joiner is a specialty tool used with glue and biscuits to make strong joints between two sections of some types of countertops.
- A reciprocating saw is ideal for removing old cabinets and countertops quickly and with a minimum of sweat—or cutting wall studs when necessary.
- A compound power miter saw has a head that pivots to cut both bevels and miters, and produces pro-quality precision cuts. Sliding miter saws have more cutting capacity but are less portable. A fine-tooth carbide-tipped blade is best for most cabinetry and countertop materials.
- A belt sander is not essential, but can come in handy for quickly removing countertop material.

- Random orbit sanders are the tool of choice to smooth wood and other countertop and cabinet surfaces for a final finish. They don't leave circular markings as disc sanders do, and can sand in any direction regardless of wood grain.
- Finish sanders (also called palm sanders) are available in a variety of sizes and shapes for different light sanding applications. They're best for final sanding because they are slow and labor intensive.
- A table saw is the best tool for ripping stock to width, and larger models can be fitted with a molding head for cutting profiles.
- A router (plunge router is shown here) is crucial for putting detailed profiles on the outside edges of countertops and for cleaning up the surfaces of other cuts.

Jobsite Preparation

Whether you are installing elaborate, custom, wall-mounted cabinets or a very basic freestanding cabinet with built-in countertop, preparing the jobsite will be crucial to making the project as easy and efficient as possible. Remove furniture and other possible obstructions from the room you will be working in so that you won't worry about getting sawdust on your brand new kitchen table or all over your nice tile floor. Cover surfaces and fixtures with plastic sheeting and protect vulnerable floors with cardboard or dropcloths, to protect them from scratches and make clean-up easier.

Set up tools such as a power miter saw at a central workstation, to avoid walking long distances between where you are installing and where you are cutting material. This central location is key to professional results because measurements are easier to remember and quick trimming is possible without the added time of exiting and entering the house.

Make sure the work area is well lit. If you don't already own one, purchase a portable light (trouble light) to make viewing the work pieces easier. Keep your tools sharp and clean. Accidents are more likely when blades are dull and tools are covered in dust and dirt.

Keep the work area clean and organized. A dedicated table or set aside part of the floor can be used as a staging platform to organize your tools and materials, and instructions as necessary. A tool table or staging area ensures that tools and equipment don't disappear, and that they are always at hand when you need them. Add a set of clamps to the table and you have a convenient space for fine-tuning the fit of each piece.

A staging area or large, dedicated work table is the perfect place to organize tools and materials so that you can find them when you need them, protect them from damage, and avoid wearing a tool belt.

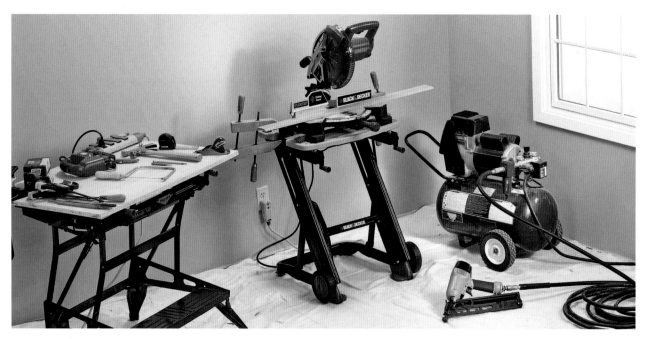

Larger cabinet and countertop installations are best approached by converting the entire room into a temporary workshop, making sure to protect all the surfaces in the space.

Project Safety

Personal safety should be priority one when working with cabinets and countertops. The power tools and hand tools you'll use to install these fixtures have the potential to cause serious injuries. That's why the first rule of project safety is to be prepared for any accident by keeping a properly stocked first aid kit nearby. Equip your kit with a variety of bandage sizes and other necessary items such as antiseptic wipes, cotton swabs, tweezers, sterile gauze, and a first aid handbook.

To help you avoid using that kit, read the owner's manuals for all power tools before operating them, and follow all the recommended precautions. Most tool-related injuries occur from improper or outright misuse of the tool. Never modify the guards on power tools, or use a tool on a job for which it wasn't designed. Protect yourself with safety glasses, ear protection, and dust masks and respirators as necessary.

It's all a matter of getting into good work habits. Speed is the enemy of safety and can lead to fabrication and installation mistakes as well as injury. Don't work when you're tired and keep your work environment clean and free of clutter. Clean your tools and put them away after each work session, sweep up dust and any leftover fasteners, and collect scraps of cut-off trim in a work bucket. These scraps may come in handy before the end of the project, so keep them around until you're finished.

Keep safety in mind and you'll not only wind up with cabinets and countertops to be proud of, but you'll have gotten there injury free.

Safety Tip ▶

Always wear safety glasses and ear protection when operating power tools. Use dust masks when necessary, and protect yourself from toxic chemicals with a respirator. Work gloves save your hands when moving or handling large and unwieldy cabinets and countertops. Kneepads are useful when working on floor-level projects, such as baseboard.

Read the owner's manual before operating any power tool. Your tools may differ in many ways from those described in this book, so it's best to familiarize yourself with the features and capabilities of the tools you own. Always wear eye and ear protection when operating a power tool. Wear a dust mask when the project will produce dust.

CABINETS

The fact that cabinets can be neatly divided into two categories—face-frame and frameless—belies the incredible diversity of cabinet styles. Cabinets tend to dominate the look of the rooms in which they are installed, so it's fortunate that you can find cabinets in modern, contemporary, traditional, country, funky, and even historical period designs. Where cabinets are concerned, there really is a look for every homeowner and every home.

Once you get past that decision of whether you want a frameless or framed cabinet (really, whether you want a bit more storage and accessibility), you'll be deciding on stock, semi-custom, or fully custom units. Stock units derive their name from being "in-stock" at the retail store. This means that there is a more limited set of color and design options among stock cabinets, but the number of options continues to grow along with the potential outlets where you can buy these cabinets. Semi-custom offers a bit more flexibility, allowing you to swap features in and out of stock cases and door sets, while custom means just that—a new set of cabinets built to your specs and tastes.

Regardless of which you choose, the most exciting areas of innovation among cabinets on the market is the development of increasingly specialized storage features. These allow you to introduce pantry elements within your new cabinets—you can add pull-out spice racks, lid organizers, tiered "stadium" storage features, and many more. Put some thought into the cabinets you select and the special features they contain, and you'll wind up with a wonderful design element that adds immeasurably to the look and function of a room.

Cabinet Selection

Buying new cabinets involves more decisions than just the look of the cabinet. First, you need to decide if you want to go with stock, semi-custom, or custom cabinets. Then you need to choose between face-frame and frameless styles. Those decisions will, in turn, lead to decisions on doors, drawers, accessories, hardware, and finishes.

Stock cabinets and some semi-custom cabinets are manufactured and intended for homeowners to install themselves; custom cabinets usually are installed by the cabinetmaker. There's a growing trend in "unfitted" kitchen systems, too. Seen most frequently in European kitchens, the cabinets and shelves are modular—like pieces of storage furniture—rather than built-in or fitted.

Stock

Stock cabinets are available as either ready-to-assemble (RTA) or ready-to-install. Ready-to-assemble cabinets, also referred to as knockdown or flat-pack, are shipped as flat components that the consumer puts together using connecting hardware. In other words, in addition to installing the cabinets, you have to assemble them. Your options will be somewhat limited if you choose RTA cabinets, but you will be able to achieve a slightly different look from ready-to-install cabinets. RTA cabinets are known for their low price points. However, although some RTA cabinets are made with low-quality materials, not all are poorly constructed. Carefully inspect samples of assembled cabinets to check material and engineering quality. If possible, also look at assembly directions to check for clarity.

Ready-to-install cabinets are purchased already assembled. They tend to be lower quality, but typical utility units are suitable for a workshop or a weekend home. Larger home centers will generally carry a limited selection of ready-to-install units, usually made from a relatively economical species of wood, such as red oak, or finished with a color layer such as white melamine.

Semi-Custom

Semi-custom cabinets are also factory-made to standard sizes, but they offer far more options in finish, size, features, and materials than you'll find in stock cabinets. Semi-custom is the best choice for homeowners who want better-quality cabinets with some special features and a custom look, but at a lower price than true custom cabinetry. You should allow at least three to eight weeks of lead time when ordering semi-custom cabinets.

Custom

Custom cabinets give the most flexibility in design, appearance, and special features. These cabinets are designed, built, and installed to fit a unique space. It is wise to shop around before settling on a custom cabinetmaker because price, quality, and availability vary widely. The minimum lead time for custom cabinet construction is six weeks in most markets. When you get bids, find out if the lead time is from acceptance of the bid or from when the condition of the kitchen allows the cabinetmaker to take accurate measurements. Remember that exotic or difficult-to-machine materials and intricate custom designs will end up costing you more and taking more time to deliver.

Standard Cabinet Sizes ▸

Base cabinets (without countertop)
Height	34½"
Depth	24"
Width	6" to 42", in 3" increments

Wall cabinets
Height	12", 15", 18", 24", 30", 36"
Depth	12"
Width	6" to 36", in 3" increments

Oven cabinets
Height	83", 95"
Depth	24"
Width	30", 33"

Pantry cabinets
Height	83", 95"
Depth	24"
Width	18", 24"

Face-Frame vs. Frameless ▸

Once you have decided between factory-made or custom cabinets, you need to choose the type of cabinet: face-frame or frameless.

Face-frame cabinets have frames made of solid wood around the front of the cabinet box. Because the frame extends into the opening space, the door openings will be reduced and a certain amount of "dead" space exists within the cabinet behind the frames. The hinges for doors on face-frame cabinets mount on the frame. The door itself may be flush within the frame or raised above it. Flush-fitting doors were common on older cabinets. But because they require a precise fit, which means more time and craftsmanship, they will be more expensive and more difficult to find.

Frameless cabinets are often referred to as "Euro-style." These cabinets do not have a face-frame and the doors and drawers span the entire width of the carcass, which allows easier access and a bit more storage space. The doors are mounted using cup hinges that are invisible when the doors are closed. Frameless cabinets have a streamlined look that makes them feel more contemporary in style. One drawback of frameless cabinets is that they do not have the added strength of the face frame, so it is critical that they are solidly constructed and properly installed.

Face-frame cabinets have openings that are completely surrounded by face frames made of vertical stiles and horizontal rails. They give kitchens a traditional look and are the most common style used in bathrooms.

Frameless cabinets, sometimes called "European-style," are more contemporary. Because they have no face frames, frameless cabinets offer slightly more storage space than framed cabinets. That's why they are also commonly used in laundry rooms and for utility spaces, such as a garage or storage area.

Cabinet Door Mounting Styles

The appearance of any cabinet's doors largely sets the tone for the overall look of the cabinets. Not only are doors, like the cabinet cases themselves, distinguished by the wood used and how it is finished, cabinet doors can also look very different depending on how they are mounted on the cabinets and the construction of the door itself. Doors are mounted in one of three ways: overlay, inset, or partial inset.

- **Overlay** doors are mounted in front of the face frame, partially or completely obscuring the face frame. Frameless overlay doors conceal the cabinet case wall edges. Full overlay doors are a contemporary look, with a streamlined appearance in which the style and finish of the doors themselves dominates the appearance of the cabinets.
- **Inset** doors are mounted between the inside edges of the face frame or within the cabinet case sides on a frameless cabinet. Consequently, the face frame or cabinet case edges are fully visible. This is a somewhat busier look because the face frame—including the joint seams—are entirely visible. It's also the least efficient mounting method in terms of accessible storage.
- **Partial inset** cabinet doors have a lip that partially conceals the face frame, while the body of the door is inset between the face frame edges. This was once a popular style, but because fabrication and installation of partial inset doors requires a greater level of craftsmanship, adding to the expense of the cabinets, this style has fallen out of favor.

Hinge Styles

Cabinet door hinges come in an astounding number of variations, but can be broken into concealed, semi-concealed, and decorative surface mounted. The cabinet door style you've chosen may determine which hinge is best—or which you can and cannot use—but in most cases, you'll have a choice of hinges. Also be aware that the cabinet material may influence your choice of hinge. For instance, if you've opted for the lower cost of particle board or MDF cabinet cases,

A concealed hinge like this can usually be adjusted in three directions, and many contain a self-closing feature that will pull the door shut by itself.

you'll most likely want to use a type of surface-mounted hinge, because cutting mortises in the material would be problematic. You'll also find specialty hinges, such as extension hinges for opening the door in a wider arc than normal, which can be a big help in a busy kitchen or on an especially deep cabinet.

Concealed hinges are just that, invisible when the door is closed. These are most often used on modern or frameless cabinets because they reinforce the sleek look established by those door styles. Most concealed hinges are surface mounted, making them easy to install because they don't require cutting a mortise. These are usually adjustable as well, allowing you to fine-tune the door fit in three directions without much expertise or specialized tools.

Semi-concealed hinges are also known as inset hinges because they are most commonly used for inset doors (you'll find variations for use with partial inset doors). In most cases, these hinges are simple "butt" hinges, with a central post and two tongues pivoting off the post. The tongues are usually mortised into the door on one side, and the face frame or cabinet case on the other. The pin is usually visible.

Decorative hinges can be surface mounted or mortised, but the idea is the same—to show both the pin and the tongues of the hinge. Decorative hinges are mostly reserved for period-style or themed décor cabinets (such as a country kitchen).

Cabinet Door Construction Styles

No matter how they are mounted, the actual appearance of a cabinet door is determined by the way it is constructed. There are three basic types of cabinet door: flat (or recessed) panel, raised panel, and slab or "flat front" doors. Each is associated with specific décor styles, and costs vary widely between the three styles. Specialty units, such as those with louvers or glass fronts, constitute a fourth group known as accent doors. Because they are usually more expensive than other versions, these are best used sparingly to offset a wall full of more standard cabinet fronts.

- Raised panel. These are some of the most common cabinet door styles because they suit a wide range of room design styles, from traditional to contemporary. The center panel is raised up (in reality, there is usually a recess or miter between the outer frame of the door and the inner panel). The complexity in construction makes these some of the most expensive doors on the market.

- Recessed panel. A plainer look than raised panel doors, this style features a center section that is lower than the surrounding frame of the door—often just a flat section in the middle of the door. The transitional border between the frame and the center of the door can be a detailed profile molding, but is more often left plain. The look is clean and streamlined, making this an obvious choice for modern or contemporary rooms.

- Slab. Flat-front cabinet doors are simpler to construct, which is why they are associated with lower cost cabinetry. But flat-front doors are also a key part of the "European" look, defined by clean lines and an uncomplicated appearance.

Flat-front panels are common on less expensive cabinetry, but the sleek style also finds a home on high-end modern units, such as the boldly colored cabinets in this kitchen.

The details of raised panel cabinet doors shows best with a dark finish that emphasizes the edge profile of the central panel. As this kitchen shows, it's a sophisticated look that adds immensely to the room's appeal.

Recessed panel doors present a stately look. They feature a timeless simplicity that makes this style appropriate for a wide range of room designs.

Recessed panels allow for special details such as the curved decorative inserts that grace the doors on these elegant dining room base cabinets.

Create Your Drawings

Use the icons shown here and ¼" graph paper to create drawings for your new kitchen. Use a scale of ½"= 1 ft. (1 square = 6") when drawing your plans; the icons are drawn to match this scale.

Plan view (overhead) templates for 24"-deep base cabinets

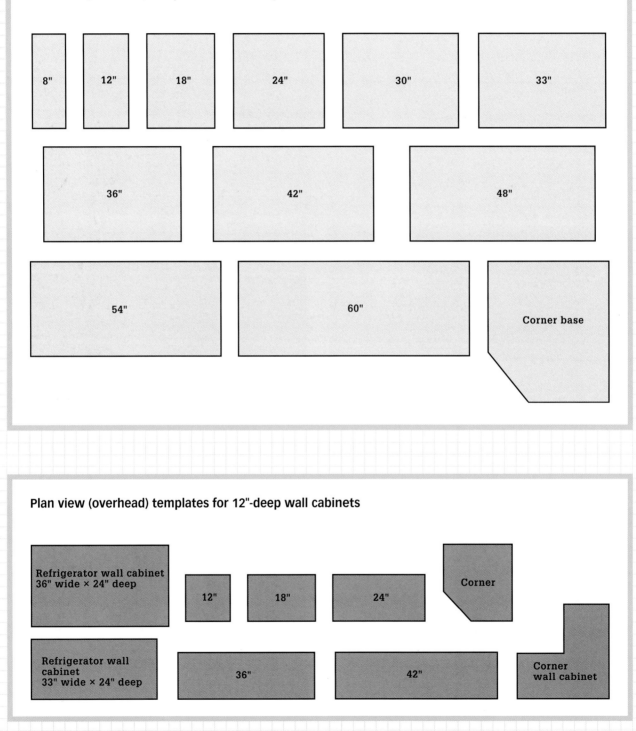

Plan view (overhead) templates for 12"-deep wall cabinets

Universal Design

Design your kitchen around a clear, circular space of at least 5 ft. in diameter to provide room for a wheelchair. If your kitchen doesn't have 60" of clear space, allow 48" for pathways. Plan for 30 to 48" of clear approach space in front of all appliances and workstations.

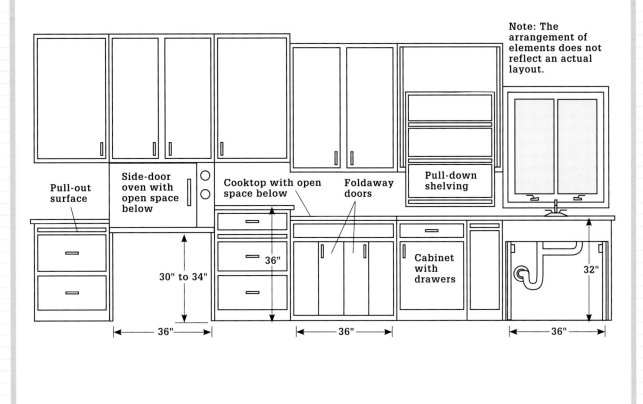

Note: The arrangement of elements does not reflect an actual layout.

Pull-out surface

Side-door oven with open space below

Cooktop with open space below

Foldaway doors

Pull-down shelving

Pull-down shelving

30" to 34"

36"

Cabinet with drawers

32"

36"

36"

36"

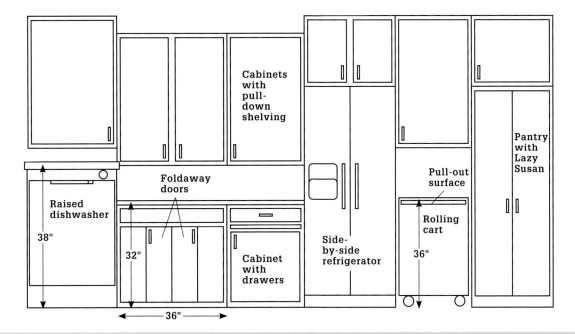

Cabinets with pull-down shelving

Foldaway doors

Raised dishwasher

38"

32"

Cabinet with drawers

Side-by-side refrigerator

Pull-out surface

Rolling cart

36"

Pantry with Lazy Susan

36"

New Cabinet Prep

Installing new cabinets is easiest if the space—preferably the whole room—is completely empty. Where appropriate and possible, disconnect plumbing and wiring, and temporarily remove the appliances and any other fixtures that are not built in. Remove old cabinets and countertops as necessary. If the new installation will require plumbing or electrical changes, now is the time to have that work done. If the flooring is to be replaced, finish it before beginning the layout and the installation of cabinets.

No matter where you put them, cabinets must be installed plumb and level. Using a level as a guide, draw reference lines on the walls to indicate cabinet location. If the floor is uneven, find the highest point of the floor area that will be covered by base cabinets. Measure up from this point to draw reference lines.

Because cabinets call for precise installation, detail-oriented preparation is key to a successful final appearance and function. This is one of those projects for which the advice, "Measure twice, cut once," is especially applicable. Take care at this stage, and you'll be ensuring a smooth process for the rest of the installation.

Filled-in low area

Tools & Materials ▸

Stud finder	Marking pencil
Pry bar	Tape measure
Trowel	1 × 3 boards
Putty knife	Straight 6- to 8-ft.-long
Screwdriver	2 × 4
Straightedge	Wallboard compound
Level	2½" wallboard screws

Stud locations

1 × 3
ledger

Reference
line

Removing Old Cabinets

Old cabinets can be salvaged fairly easily if they are modular units that were installed with screws. Some custom built-in cabinets can be removed in one piece. If you're not planning on salvaging the cabinets, they should be cut into pieces or otherwise broken down and discarded. If you're demolishing your old cabinets, you still need to exercise caution to prevent causing collateral damage in the room, especially to existing plumbing and electrical lines.

Tools & Materials ▸

Tape measure	Reciprocating saw
Pry bar	Hammer
Putty knife	Eye protection
Cordless screwdriver	Scrap wood
Sander	2 × 4
Stud finder	Wallboard compound
Taping knife	1 × 3 lumber
Level	2½" wallboard screws
Laser level	

How to Remove Cabinets

Remove trim moldings at the edges and tops of the cabinets with a flat pry bar or putty knife.

Remove base shoe from cabinet base if the molding is attached to the floor.

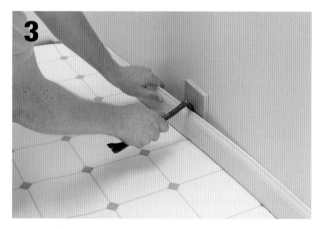

Remove baseboards and other trim moldings with a pry bar. Protect wall surfaces with scraps of wood. Label the baseboards and trim on the back so you can replace them correctly.

Remove valances above cabinets. Some valances are attached to the cabinets or soffits with screws. Others are nailed and must be pried loose.

5

High-end countertops such as marble or granite should be carefully separated from the tops of the cabinets. Less expensive countertops are usually not salvageable. Cut them into manageable pieces with a reciprocating saw, or take them apart, piece by piece, with a hammer and pry bar.

6

Remove doors and drawers to make it easier to get at interior spaces. You may need to scrape away old paint to expose hinge screws and other fasteners.

7

At the backs of cabinets, remove any screws holding the cabinet to the wall. Cabinets can be removed as a group or can be disassembled.

8

Detach individual cabinets by removing screws that hold face frames together. You may need to unscrew other attachment screws in the sides of cabinets.

How to Prepare Walls

1

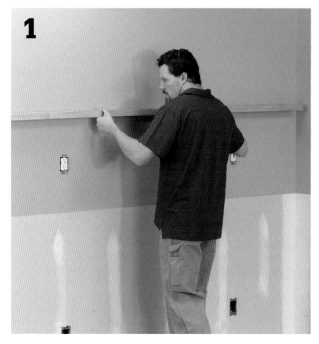

Find high and low spots on wall surfaces using a long, straight 2 × 4. Sand down any high spots.

2

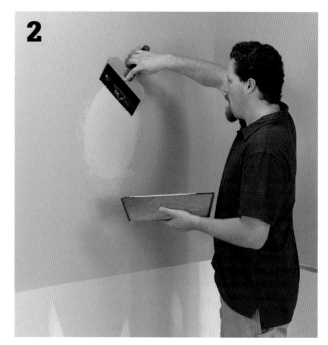

Fill in low spots in the wall by applying drywall joint compound with a taping knife. Feather edges carefully. Let the compound dry, and then sand lightly.

3

Locate and mark wall studs using an electronic stud finder. Cabinets normally will be hung by driving screws into the studs through the back of the cabinets.

4

Find the highest point along the floor that will be covered by base cabinets. Place a level on a long, straight 2 × 4, and move the board across the floor to determine if the floor is uneven. Mark the wall at the highest point.

5

Measure up 34½" from the high-point mark (for standard cabinets). Use a level (a laser level is perfect) to mark a reference line on the walls. Base cabinets will be installed with the top edges flush against this line.

6

Measure up 84" from the high-point mark and draw a second reference line. Wall cabinets will be installed with their top edges flush against this line.

7

Measure down 30" from the wall-cabinet reference line and draw another level line where the bottoms of the cabinets will be. Temporary ledgers will be installed against this line.

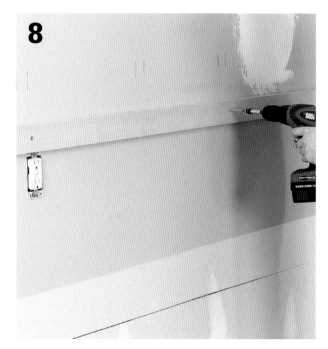

8

Install 1 × 3 temporary ledgers with top edges flush against the reference lines. Attach ledgers with 2½" wallboard screws driven into every other wall stud. Mark stud locations on the ledgers. Cabinets will rest temporarily on ledgers during installation (the ledgers alone will not support them, however).

Stock Cabinets

When budget is your chief concern, you'll probably be shopping for stock cabinetry. These are sometimes called "in-stock" cabinets because they are the standard units that home centers and other stores either keep on hand or in a warehouse deliverable within a day or two. These days, the design options among stock cabinets are more varied than they once were, but they are still more limited than what you'll find among semi-custom or custom units.

What you give up in style choices with stock cabinets, you gain in standardization. They are usually offered in widths ranging from 1 foot to up to 5 feet wide, in increments of 1 or 3 inches. This means you will need to use filler strips when the gap between a cabinet and a wall or fixture is less than the minimum cabinet increment for the units you are buying. Heights vary from 30 inches up to 36 inches tall (34 ½ inches tall by 24 inches deep is standard). Smaller units are also available for specialized locations, such as over a stove. This uniformity can make laying out a full kitchen installation easy, but

it also makes stock cabinets ideal for more unusual spaces such as laundry rooms or mud rooms. The more modest quality of many stock units will also not be so apparent in these types of utilitarian spaces.

Stock cabinets are often frameless, a reflection of inexpensive production costs. But you can also find face-frame units on the higher end of the spectrum, and even special features like pull-out spice racks and solid wood doors.

No matter what extra features you choose, however, you want stock cabinets to be solidly built and durable. Signs of quality are the same regardless of price point.

- **Dovetailed drawers** ensure that these high-use features won't fall apart before the cabinets do. Drawer boxes constructed of solid wood are a sure sign of high-quality stock cabinetry.
- **Plywood** is an indicator of rugged cabinet boxes. Many lower-end stock cabinets are constructed with particle board or MDF, with a very thin layer of veneer. These boxes can be a weak spot for low cost units; plywood is likely to last longer and stay in better shape over the life of the cabinets.
- **Drawer glides**, rather than just channels or wood guides, are a true sign of quality in stock cabinetry. Although they may not make a big difference in the look of the cabinets, metal drawer glides allow the drawers to hold up better to wear and tear over time, and make it much less frustrating to use the drawers.
- **The extras.** Additional features can indicate a better quality stock cabinet. Glass inserts, special moldings and kick plates, decorative corbels or faux feet are all signs of stock cabinets that aspire to semi-custom quality.
- **Warranties and guarantees** are also fairly reliable gauges of how durable the cabinets will be over time and use. The better and tougher the construction, the longer the company will back up the cabinets. At the lower end of the scale, expect warranties of a year or less. Better cabinets will be warrantied for up to five years. The length of the warranty usually directly relates to the durability of the cabinets.

Stock cabinets are sold in boxes that are keyed to door and drawer packs (you need to buy these separately). It is important that you realize this when you are estimating your project costs (often a door pack will cost as much or more than the cabinet itself).

Working with Stock Cabinets

You have to honestly assess your abilities when shopping for stock cabinetry. Although they don't really require much skill, ready-to-assemble units take a little work and an attention to detail to fabricate. If you aren't thrilled about tackling assembly, you can choose ready-to-install units. Although assembly requires only moderate DIY skills, be prepared to spend nearly an hour on each run of base or wall-mounted cabinets. As with all cabinet installations, patience and attention to detail are crucial to good-looking results.

Stock cabinets can tend toward plain, but that doesn't mean that they're ugly. These modest units show that the right stock cabinets in the right space can create a clean, streamlined, and handsome look. Especially when coupled with granite countertops and stainless-steel appliances. The right stock units can add immeasurably to a laundry room or other utility or work space (inset).

Wall-Mounted Cabinets

No matter where they are installed, wall-mounted cabinets are a great way to use vertical space. In a kitchen, they supply ample room for dry goods on a wall above a countertop. Bathroom wall cabinets are your chance to expand storage for toilet paper and other essentials without taking up precious floor space. Laundry room wall-mounted cabinets put cleaning supplies right at fingertips, making an unappealing chore less so.

As with other types of cabinets, installing wall cabinets is a matter of precision. When mounting a cabinet or row of cabinets at eye level, errors are magnified. That's why it's a good rule of thumb to always install wall-mounted cabinets before you put base cabinets in place, or install any floor-mounted fixtures. Having plenty of room to move around is one way to head off any potential mistakes.

The instructions in the pages that follow focus on surface-mounted units. When you're installing a medicine chest or any cabinetry that requires inset installation, follow the manufacturer's directions—and basic safety procedures such as checking the wall cavities for electrical lines running inside walls.

In any case, double-check that no vents, outlets, or other essential features will be blocked by the installation of a wall cabinet. You'll want to reference

local codes regarding the proper distance between the bottom of wall-mounted cabinets and heat sources such as a range top. We also suggest setting out a run of wall-mounted cabinets along the wall before installation, to check measurements, fit, and visualize any problems or challenges. On bigger jobs such as installing wall cabinets for a large kitchen, mark the cabinets with notes referencing their relative positions, by using a marker and painter's tape.

Tools & Materials ▸

Handscrew clamps	Toe-kick molding
Level	Filler strips
Hammer	Valance
Utility knife	6d finish nails
Nail set	Finish washers
C-clamps	2 ½", 4" wood screws
Power drill	2 ½" cabinet screws or
Counterbore drill bit	flathead wood screws
Phillips screwdriver	Sheet-metal screws
1 x 3 lumber	#8 panhead wood screws
Cabinets	3" drywall screws
Trim molding	Shims

The right wall cabinets in the right place can provide a surprising amount of extra storage, such as the upper cabinets in this entryway system. Using wall cabinets that match the rest of the structure maintains a unified design that makes the space look sharp.

How to Install Wall Cabinets

Position a corner upper cabinet on a ledger and hold it in place, making sure it is resting cleanly on the ledger. Drill ³⁄₁₆" pilot holes into the wall studs through the hanging strips at the top rear of the cabinet. Attach the cabinet to the wall with 2½" screws. Do not tighten fully until all cabinets are hung.

Attach a filler strip to the front edge of the cabinet, if needed (see page 38). Clamp the strip in place and drill counterbored pilot holes through the cabinet face frame near hinge locations. Attach the filler strip to cabinet with 2½" cabinet screws or flathead wood screws.

Position the adjoining cabinet on the ledger, tight against the corner cabinet or filler strip. Clamp the corner cabinet and the adjoining cabinet together at the top and bottom. Handscrew clamps will not damage wood face frames.

Check the front cabinet edges or face frames for plumb. Drill ³⁄₁₆" pilot holes into the wall studs through the hanging strips in the rear of the cabinet. Attach the cabinet with 2½" screws. Do not tighten the wall screws fully until all the cabinets are hung.

(continued)

Attach the corner cabinet to the adjoining cabinet. From the inside corner cabinet, drill pilot holes through the case. Join the cabinets with sheet-metal screws.

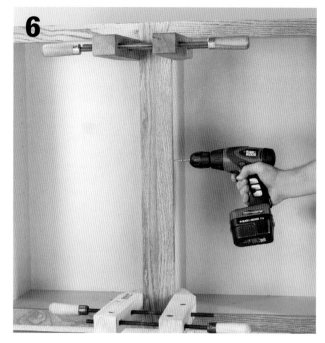

Position and attach each additional cabinet. Clamp the frames together, and drill counterbored pilot holes through the side of the frame. Join the cabinets with wood screws. Drill ³⁄₁₆" pilot holes in the hanging strips, and attach the cabinet to the studs with wood screws.

Join the cabinets with #8 × 1¼" panhead wood screws or wood screws with decorative washers. Each pair of cabinets should be joined by at least four screws.

Fill the gaps between the cabinet and wall or neighboring appliance with a filler strip. Cut the filler strip to fit the space, then wedge wood shims between the filler strip and the wall to create a friction fit that holds it in place temporarily. Drill counterbored pilot holes through the side of the cabinet (or the edge of the face frame) and attach the filler with screws.

9

Remove the temporary ledger. Check the cabinet run for plumb, and adjust if necessary by placing wood shims behind the cabinet, near the stud locations. Tighten the wall screws completely. Cut off the shims with a utility knife.

10

Use trim moldings to cover any gaps between the cabinets and the walls. Stain the moldings to match the cabinet finish.

11

Attach a decorative valance above the sink. Clamp the valance to the edge of cabinet frames and drill counterbored pilot holes through the cabinet frames and into the end of the valance. Attach with sheet-metal screws.

12

Install the cabinet doors. If necessary, adjust the hinges so that the doors are straight and plumb.

Base Cabinets

Base cabinets can serve as the foundation for a room's design, especially in the kitchen or bathroom. Today's base cabinets are much more than simple storage boxes; they can be outfitted with a vast range of specialized features to accommodate extremely specific storage needs. More and more stock cabinets are being offered with these features (and can easily be retrofitted with them), including lazy Susans, pull-out spice racks, vertical inserts for plates, lids, or flat baking sheets and pans, and even specialized drawers designed to hold makeup or cutlery.

But no matter what features you've chosen, the cabinets need to be installed level for everything to work correctly. You can also save yourself a lot of frustration and effort by performing any upgrades to electrical or plumbing systems before installing the cabinets.

Flooring represents an often-overlooked factor in base cabinet installation, but it's immensely important. You'll need to figure in the finished floor height in your cabinet calculations, but that height will depend on more than the flooring you've chosen for the room. Some flooring, such as linoleum, is not meant to be placed under installed cabinetry because the material needs to expand and contract. Most other flooring materials should be run under the cabinets.

Just as it's easier to install most final flooring before installing the base cabinets, it's also wise to check the location of plumbing and electrical lines and connections before attaching base cabinets to wall surfaces. You'll need to cut the appropriate openings for these connections, but you'll also need to accommodate the placement and installation of features such as sinks, faucets, and dishwasher lines that run through cabinet sidewalls.

As much as possible, test-fit fixtures and features before installing the base cabinets. You'll want to know that there is room for the sink to fit into the top of the base cabinet, but this will also give you a chance to determine the order of installation. For instance, it may be wiser to install a faucet before installing the sink, if the sink is so deep that it will make for a difficult time getting to the nuts on the underside of the faucet. The more you can troubleshoot issues like this, the more likely your base cabinets will go in without a hitch.

Obviously, there are a lot of variables involved with base cabinet installation. But work through the process one logical step at a time, and you'll find that the skills needed are actually fairly modest. Just about anyone who can handle a power drill and jigsaw can install a set of base cabinets in a day.

Base cabinets come in many sizes and shapes, but they all share certain common traits. The cabinets under this window seat were installed just as kitchen base cabinets would be, with doors and a toe-kick plate that mimics those found on kitchen base cabinets.

1

2

Begin the installation with a corner cabinet. Draw plumb lines that intersect the 34½" reference line (measured from the high point of the floor) at the locations for the cabinet sides.

Place the cabinet in the corner. Make sure the cabinet is plumb and level. If necessary, adjust by driving wood shims under the cabinet base. Be careful not to damage the flooring. Drill ³⁄₁₆" pilot holes through the hanging strip and into the wall studs. Tack the cabinet to the wall with wood screws or wallboard screws.

3

4

Clamp the adjoining cabinet to the corner cabinet. Make sure the new cabinet is plumb, then drill counterbored pilot holes through the cabinet sides or the face frame and filler strip. Screw the cabinets together. Drill ³⁄₁₆" pilot holes through the hanging strips and into the wall studs. Tack the cabinets loosely to the wall studs with wood screws or wallboard screws.

Use a jigsaw to cut any cabinet openings needed in the cabinet backs (for example, in the sink base seen here) for plumbing, wiring, or heating ducts.

(continued)

Position and attach additional cabinets, making sure the frames are aligned and the cabinet tops are level. Clamp cabinets together, then attach the face frames or cabinet sides with screws driven into pilot holes. Tack the cabinets to the wall studs, but don't drive screws too tight—you may need to make adjustments once the entire bank is installed.

Make sure all the cabinets are level. If necessary, adjust by driving shims underneath the cabinets. Place the shims behind the cabinets near the stud locations to fill any gaps. Tighten the wall screws. Cut off the shims with a utility knife.

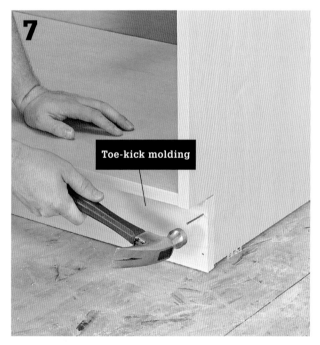

Toe-kick molding

Use trim moldings to cover gaps between the cabinets and the wall or floor. The toe-kick area is often covered with a strip of wood finished to match the cabinets or painted black.

Hang the cabinet doors and mount the drawer fronts, then test to make sure they close smoothly and the doors fit evenly and flush. Self-closing cabinet hinges (by far the most common type installed today) have adjustment screws that allow you to make minor changes to the hardware to correct any problems.

Adjusting European Hinges ▸

European hinges (also called cup hinges) are the standard hinges used on frameless cabinets and some face-frame cabinets. One advantage of these hinges is their adjustability. This adjustability means that you will need some patience to tackle this project.

At first glance, European hinges appear to need a Phillips screwdriver to be adjusted, but you will have more success if you use a Pozidrive #2 screwdriver. This looks like a Phillips driver, but it is engineered with extra blade tips for reduced slippage. Never use a power screwdriver for hinge adjustments.

European hinges have three adjustment screws that secure the hinge to the door and cabinet while moving the door in and out, up and down, or right to left. If you own face-frame cabinets, the hinges may be more compact than frameless cabinet hinges. Some of the most compact hinges have unique adjustment systems, so you may have more trial and error in installing them.

Before making any adjustments, try tightening the anchoring screw or the vertical adjustment screws. Often these screws have worked loose over time and are affecting the door alignment and function.

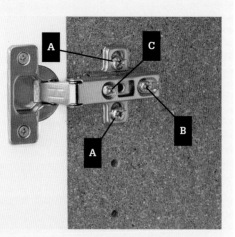

Long-arm European hinges. The standard long-arm European hinge has four adjustment screws. The first pair (A) attach to the mounting plate to the side of the cabinet. Loosen these screws slightly on both hinges to move the cabinet up and down vertically. Retighten the screws when you have the hinge aligned as desired. The third adjustment screw (B) attaches the hinge to the mounting plate. If this screw is loose, the door will move in and out and seem floppy. This screw should be in the same relative position in its slot as the B screw on the other hinge, and they should both always be tight. The fourth screw (C) adjusts the door left and right horizontally. Adjust one hinge at a time in small increments by turning the screw. Check the adjustment results frequently by closing the door.

European hinges. Cabinet doors with European hinges can be adjusted in three dimensions: vertical (up and down) (A); depth (in and out) (B); and horizontal (right and left) (C). If your cabinets are slightly out of alignment, begin door installation with the center cabinet and work your way out to one side and then the other.

Compact European hinges. The compact European hinge for overlay doors on face-frame cabinets has three adjustment screws. The first pair (A) attach to the mounting clip to the side or front of the face frame. Screws B and C attach the hinge to the mounting plate and serve as the left and right adjustment. Loosen all the A screws slightly to adjust the door up or down, then tighten. Loosen or tighten one B or C screw in small increments to move the door left or right. Check the adjustment results frequently by closing the door.

Frameless Cabinetry

Understanding frameless cabinetry means understanding a bit of history. Prior to the late 1950s, the only type of cabinets mass produced in America were those built with face frames. That was the traditional style of construction dating from the turn of the century, when cabinets were hand crafted. As they geared up for mass production, manufacturers tooled their operations to produce face-frame cabinetry, and that's about all you could find until European vendors—most notably IKEA—began marketing in America.

That history is why face-frame cabinetry still dominates the American marketplace (over 80 percent of the cabinets sold in America today are framed), and why the selection of frameless cabinets is somewhat more limited than the options among face-frame units. Fortunately, the frameless style continues to grow in popularity, and more frameless designs are available than ever before.

Early frameless cabinets were low-end units, usually reserved for utility spaces such as laundry rooms, garages, and college dorm rooms. The selection has expanded greatly since then, and today you'll find sleek, modern stock frameless cabinets well-suited to a high-end kitchen remodel.

In fact, as the frameless cabinets have become more popular, their look has evolved and become identifiable in its own right. Most frameless cabinets feature a clean, streamlined look that is called "European," a nod to the origin of the construction style. The look also translates very well to high-end contemporary and modern decors, where frameless cabinets just naturally fit into the uncluttered aesthetic. Frameless cabinets are often fitted with flat-front "slab doors" that reinforce the look, and make it ideal for presenting bold colors such as red and lime green.

On the functional side, frameless cabinets offer storage that is a bit easier to access because there is no lip around the front edge of the cabinet to block reaching into the interior—as there is on a face-framed unit. This is a nice extra that makes it that much simpler to slide plates and heavy objects in and out of the cabinets. It also means one less area where dirt can be trapped.

Frameless cabinets are installed in pretty much the same way, and with the same tools, that framed cabinets are. However, attaching doors will usually be a bit easier because you won't need to contend with the lip. In the final analysis, if the look appeals to your tastes and suits the other fixtures and features in the room, frameless cabinets can be the ideal storage option for both high-profile rooms such as the kitchen and more utilitarian spaces such as a laundry room.

Simple, understated and streamlined, frameless cabinets are a great look and easy to install in the right space.

Even a small kitchen such as this can be brought to life by the right stylish frameless cabinets. The addition of frosted glass fronts to the wall-mounted cabinets in this room puts the icing on the cake.

Freestanding Cabinets

As you shop for cabinets, you'll likely come across a type that is fairly new in America but that has been around for a long time in Europe: the freestanding cabinet. Boasting a contemporary appearance and ease of installation, these cabinets bring the added benefits of portability and interchangeability (sink base cabinets are a notable exception). Most freestanding bases come in an assortment of materials, colors, and sizes with matching upper cabinets. The upper cabinets are hung nontraditionally, usually mounting directly onto a rail that is attached to the wall, which can also support shelves and organizer bins.

Freestanding cabinets, like their permanently installed counterparts, are usually shipped and sold in flat packs. Because they are sold ready to assemble (RTA), you'll have to assemble your cabinets before installing them.

It is best to start your assembly with a basic, small cabinet. That way, you can get the knack of the process without wrestling with large pieces. Installing a freestanding kitchen cabinet system is similar to most other wall-cabinet installations. You need to begin with level wall surfaces. The cabinets are hung on a suspension rail and then bolted to the bar. The bolts, in the upper inside corners of the cabinets, are then covered with plastic caps. If you install the suspension rail properly, this type of installation ensures that your cabinets will be level. If you add toe-kick panels to your base cabinets, they will be virtually indistinguishable from fully installed base cabinets. Or, you can create a European look by installing attractive legs and leaving the toe-kick covers off. When opting for this look, cut the ledger board 5" to 6" short, and install a third leg on the exposed end cabinets so that the ledger board will not be visible. When creating an island with base cabinets, you must attach the legs to the floor to prevent movement. A sink base cabinet must also be secured to ensure that it is stationary.

Freestanding base cabinets really have more in common with furniture—including ease of installation—than cabinetry, but they serve the same important function as traditionally installed cabinets do.

European-style freestanding base cabinets are a distinctive look that naturally pair well with metals such as the stainless steel legs and sink shown in these photos, and with natural materials such as wood.

Tips for Installing Freestanding Cabinets ▸

- Carefully unpack each carton and double-check the contents against the instruction sheets.
- Use painters' tape to attach hardware packets and instructions to their respective parts.
- Check nooks and crannies of packing materials. Hardware bags are often encased in packing materials.
- Parts may be grouped—for example, the ledger boards are packed with the toe-kick boards.
- If you are assembling large cabinets in another room, make sure you have the space to move them to the kitchen when fully assembled (check room door widths).
- Make sure the proper side of the cabinet back faces the inside of the cabinet.
- Check that drawers are right side up before drilling handle holes.
- Fiberboard material is very heavy. You should have at least one helper when installing.

Freestanding base cabinets come in as wide range of styles as other types of cabinets. You'll find units with shelves, drawers, and simple cabinets.

Customizing Stock Cabinets

Even if you don't have the time or need to pursue a complete kitchen remodel, or you want to dress up the stock cabinets you've purchased, there are ways to easily freshen the look of your cabinets. Raise a single wall cabinet within a bank of cabinets to create more space for countertop appliances or simply to change the look. This tactic works especially well on corner cabinets. Or, you can convert a cabinet to open shelving and create a new display area. Adding crown molding to stock cabinets will give your whole kitchen a more finished look. You can really dress up a stock cabinet by removing a cabinet door panel and replacing it with glass, to form an enclosed display space.

Create a display cabinet from a frameless unit. If your cabinets have removable shelves, you can transform one or more of them into a display cabinet. Begin by removing the door and hinges and removing the existing shelves and shelf supports. Fill the screw holes and finish to match the cabinet exterior. Paint the inside of the cabinet with gloss enamel. Create a template with guide holes for pin-style shelf supports. Drill the holes for the shelf supports. Measure the space and order tempered glass shelves to fit.

Raise a cabinet. To raise a cabinet, remove the contents of the cabinet and the adjoining cabinets. Remove any trim or crown molding. Remove the screws holding the face frames together or the binder bolts holding the cabinet cases together in a frameless cabinet. Remove the screws holding the cabinet to the wall. Move the cabinet up 4 to 6". It is likely it will stick from paint or age. If so, use a hammer against a padded piece of 2 × 4 to persuade it to move (you'll want a helper to steady the cabinet). Reinstall the cabinet at its new height. Refinish the cabinet sides to match.

Attach crown molding. Generally, this project works best for face-frame cabinets because frameless cabinets do not have the traditional look that crown molding complements. If your cabinets have exposed sides with a lip or edge trim, you will need to remove a portion of the lip or add a ¾" wide x ⅛" trim strip to build up the side to match the lip. To remove the lip, measure down ¾" from the top of the cabinets and mark a line on the lip. Use a fine-tooth backsaw to carefully cut down to the side of the cabinet. Use a chisel to remove the upper part of the lip. Cut the longest piece of crown molding first. Measure the cabinet run from end to end. Using a compound miter saw, cut each end at 22½°. Install the molding ¾" down from the top of the cabinets. Nail the molding in place with a finish nailer (photo). Cut the end piece to fit and nail in place.

How to Install a Glass Panel Door

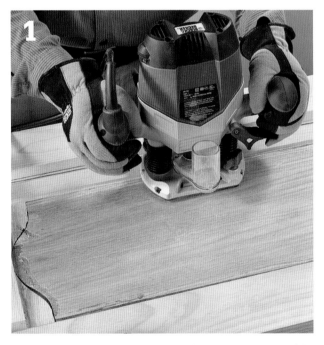

Cut a recess for a glass panel in the frame. Use a router with a straight bit to cut away the lip on the rails and stiles of the door frame. Set the router to the depth of the lip. Clamp the door to the work surface. Clamp guides to the work surface. Rout out the lip. Remove the panel. Square the corners of the cutout with a chisel.

Install the glass. Measure the cutout and order a piece of tempered glass to fit. Consider the many types of glass, including frosted and pebbled glass to coordinate with the rest of the kitchen. Use glass clips to install the glass panel. Reattach the hardware and rehang the door.

Slide-Out Storage

A base cabinet with slide-out trays or shelves is one of those great modern conveniences that has become standard in new kitchen and bathroom designs. Not only do slide-out trays make reaching stored items easier than with standard cabinet spaces—no more crouching and diving into the deep recesses of cavernous low shelves—they also store more items far more efficiently. With a few shallow trays, a standard base cabinet can hold dozens of food cans or bottles of makeup, and still leave room for tall items such as cereal boxes, cleaning supplies, bags of flour, or even pots and countertop appliances.

To get the most from your new slide-out system, think carefully about how you will use each tray. Measure the items you're most likely to store together, and let the items dictate the spacing of the trays. Most standard base cabinets are suitable for trays. Wide cabinets (24" or wider) without a center partition (middle stile) are best in terms of space usage, but trays in narrow (18"-wide) cabinets are just as handy. If you have a wide cabinet with a middle stile, you can add trays along one or both sides of the stile. For economy and simplicity, the trays in this project are made with ¾"-thick plywood parts joined with glue and finish nails. If you prefer a more finished look (not that there's anything wrong with the look of nice plywood), you can use 1 × 4 hardwood stock for the tray sides and set a ⅜"-thick plywood bottom panel into dadoes milled into the side pieces. Another option is to assemble plywood tray pieces using pocket screws so that the screw heads don't show on the front pieces of the trays.

Tools & Materials ▸

Circular saw with straightedge guide or table saw	¾" finish-grade plywood
Power drill	Wood glue
Wood screws	6d finish nails
Drawer slides (1 set per tray)	Finish materials
1 × 2 hardwood stock	Tape measure
	Varnish or polyurethane

Slide-out trays eliminate the everyday problem of hard-to-reach and hard-to-see spaces in standard base cabinets. Better still, you can install your trays to accommodate the stuff you use most often.

Drawer Slides

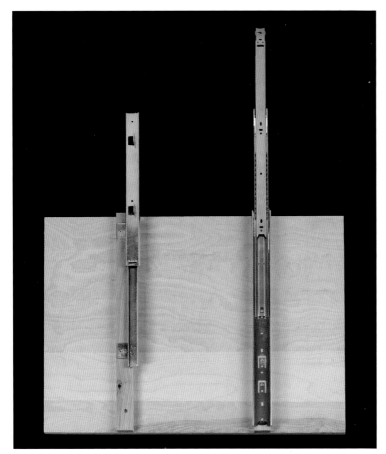

Drawer slides suitable for pull-out shelves are commonly available in both standard (left) and full extension (right) styles. Standard slides are less expensive and good enough for most applications. They allow the tray to be pulled out most of the way. Full extension slides are a little pricier than standard slides, but they allow the tray to be pulled completely out of the cabinet box for easy access to items in the back.

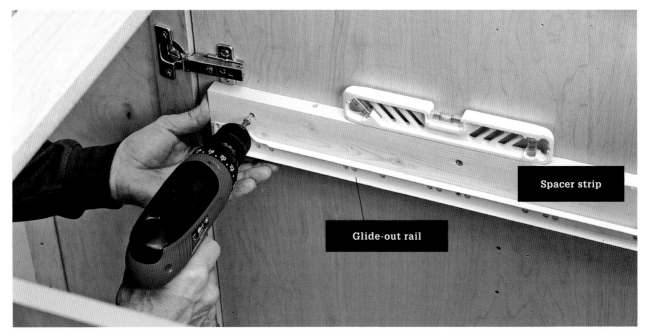

Spacer strip

Glide-out rail

Spacers must be mounted to the wall cabinets before you can install drawer slides for your slide-out shelves. They are necessary for the drawers to clear the cabinet face frame and the door (these aren't necessary for frameless cabinets). For a ¾" spacer, a 1 × 3 or 1 × 4 works well. Paint or finish it to match the cabinet interior.

How to Install Slide-Out Cabinet Trays

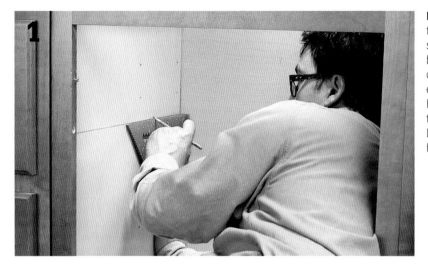

Lay out the tray positions, starting with the bottom tray. Check the drawer slides to see how much clearance you need for the bottom tray. Draw lines on the side panels of the cabinet to represent the bottom edges of the slide supports. Make sure the lines are level and are perpendicular to the cabinet front. Cut the slide supports to length from 1 × 2 hardwood stock (or any hardwood ripped to 1½" wide).

Mount the supports to the side panels of the cabinet with glue and screws driven through countersunk pilot holes. **Note:** Depending on the overhang of the cabinet face frames, you may need thicker support stock to provide sufficient clearance for the trays and slide rails.

Install the drawer slides flush with the bottom edges of the slide supports using the provided screws. Assemble the two halves of each slide, and then measure between the drawer side pieces (rails) to find the exact width of each tray. Plan the depth of the trays based on the cabinet depth.

Cut the bottom piece for each tray from ¾" plywood 1½" smaller than the planned width and depth of the finished tray. Rip three ¾"-wide pieces for the sides, front, and back of each tray. Cut the side pieces to length, equal to the depth dimension of the bottom piece. Cut the front and back pieces 1½" longer than the width of the bottom.

Build the trays with glue and 6d finish nails or pneumatic brads. Fasten the sides flush with the bottom face and front and back edges of the bottom piece, and then add the front and back pieces. Sand any rough surfaces, and finish the trays with two or three coats of polyurethane or other durable varnish. If desired, you can stain the trays prior to finishing so they match your cabinets.

Partially mount the drawer slide rails to one of the trays, following the manufacturer's directions. Test-fit the tray in the cabinet and make any necessary adjustments before completely fastening the rails. Mount the slide rails on the remaining trays and install the trays to finish the job.

Custom Cabinetry

There are two types of custom cabinets: the high-end cabinetry you can order from manufacturers to meet your exact specifications and desired look, and the type you build yourself, from scratch. Either type will involve significant expense—high-end materials are never cheap. Order from a manufacturer and you save yourself a lot of work, not to mention that a manufacturer may be able to supply a finished product that you can't make yourself. If you build your own custom cabinets, on the other hand, you'll most likely have the cabinets in place more quickly, and you'll be able to make small changes and adjustments on the fly—changes that might have been costly and time-consuming if you were ordering through a manufacturer.

You can use the methods outlined in the projects that follow to build the cabinets you envision. Unless you're an accomplished woodworker, it's always wise to start out on a simpler project, such as a wall-mounted or base cabinet that doesn't involve installation in a corner or contain any special fittings or other difficult-to-fabricate details. Once you get comfortable with the cabinet fabrication process, you can move on

Tools & Materials ▸

Electronic stud finder	Pocket screw jig
Cordless screwdriver	Wood glue
Hammer	Biscuits, splines, or dowels
Tape measure	Finish nails (1", 2", 3", 4")
Utility knife	
Router with bits (¾" straight, ¼" rabbet)	Shims
	Pin-style shelf supports
	¾" plywood
Drill and bits	1 × 3, 1 × 6, 2 × 4 lumber
Right-angle drill guide	
	1 × 3 maple or other hardwood
Pegboard scraps	
Pipe clamps	Finishing materials
Level	Drawer and door hardware
Sander	
Circular saw	Trim or base shoe molding
Power-driver screws (¾", 2 ½", 3 ½")	
	Wood putty

Cutting Sheet Goods ▸

You'll find no better combination for cutting full-sheet panels than a full-sized table saw and a helper, with the possible exception of a panel saw. But if you are working alone, it is still possible to cut full panels down to size accurately and safely using a circular saw. The main difficulty beginners encounter when cutting panels with a circular saw is that they do not adequately support the waste, so that it falls away prematurely and ruins the cut (or causes an accident). Another common mistake is to support both ends so that the area being cut binds on the saw blade as the cut is made. The solution is simply to support the entire panel along both edges with sacrificial scraps of 2 × 4. Set your saw blade to cut just slightly deeper than the thickness of the panel. The blade will score the 2 × 4s as it cuts, but they will continue to support the work piece all the way through the cut. Be sure to use a straightedge guide for your saw, and always cut with the good face down when using a circular saw.

to one-of-a-kind entry hall cabinets; a new, highly detailed bathroom vanity; or even a suite of cabinets to transform the look and function of your kitchen. Custom-building your own cabinets is not only a way to completely control the process, it's also your chance to put a signature look on your cabinetry.

In any case, the first thing to realize is that the cabinets themselves are essentially boxes. They should be constructed square, but with a little attention to the measurements, fabricating cabinet cases shouldn't try your patience or your skills.

Focus most of your attention on the cabinet door fronts and drawers—the most highly visible parts of the design. Get these right, and the end result is sure to be pleasing to the eye. If you want to take the design one step further, you can consider adding some special features such as valances, columns, or faux

feet. These draw the eye, so if you plan to add them to your cabinets, be absolutely certain you can execute them. If you have doubts, you may want to outsource those features.

When going to the time, effort, and expense of building custom cabinets, don't skimp on hardware. It's amazing how much low-quality cabinet "jewelry" can detract from high-quality construction on custom cabinetry. This is true for the hidden hardware as well. You're likely to be less satisfied with beautiful drawer fronts if the drawer sticks every time you pull it out simply because you skimped on the drawer slides.

Finally, make sure you put a lot of attention and time into the finish of your custom cabinets. This is the detail that most often separates manufacturer's products from home-fabricated units.

You can make your own features, or custom order cabinets with special touches, like the millworked columns, special-order glass inserts, and cabinets with integrated shelving that define the look of this stunning kitchen.

Exploded View of Hanging Wall Cabinet

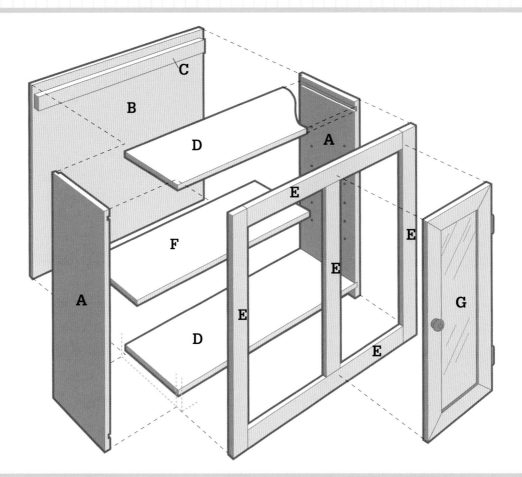

Parts List: Wall Cabinet

PROJECT AS SHOWN

KEY	PART	MATERIAL	PIECES	SIZE
A	Side panels	¾" maple plywood	2	11¼" × 30"
B	Back panel	¼" maple plywood	1	30" × 35¼"
C	Nailing strip	1 × 3 maple	1	34¼"
D	Top, bottom panels	¾" maple plywood	2	35¼ × 11¼"
E	Face frame	1 × 3 maple	12 linear ft	
F	Shelves	¾" maple plywood	2	9¾ × 34¼"
G	Glass panel or overlay doors			

Exploded View of Base Cabinet

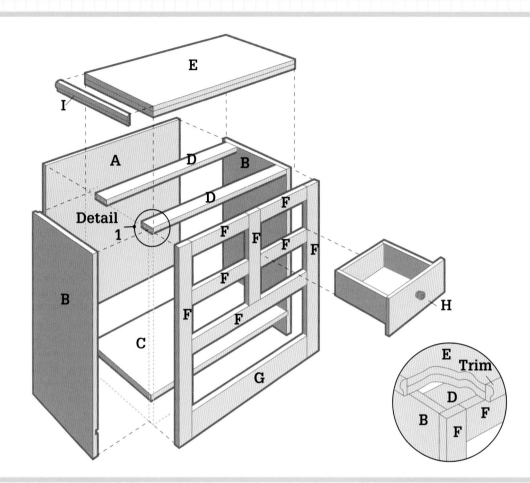

Parts List: Base Cabinet

PROJECT AS SHOWN

KEY	PART	MATERIAL	PIECES	SIZE
A	Back panel	½" maple plywood	1	34½ × 35¼"
B	Side panels	¾" maple plywood	2	34½ × 17¼"
C	Bottom panel	¾" maple plywood	1	16¾ × 35¼"
D	Supports	1 × 3 maple	2	34½"
E	Countertop	¾" plywood	2	36¼ × 18"
F	Face frame	1 × 3 maple	15 linear ft.	
G	Bottom rail	1 × 6 maple	1	31¼"
H	Overlay drawers			
I	Trim molding	12 linear ft.		

Wall Cabinet Project Details

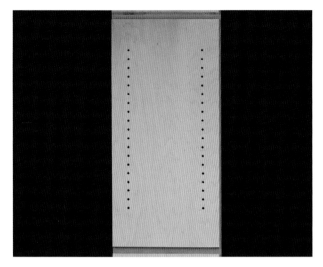

Side panels are made from ¾" plywood and have ¾"-wide, ⅜"-deep dadoes where bottom and top panels fit, and ¼"-wide rabbets where the back panel fits. Rows of parallel peg holes, 1½" in from edges, hold pin-style shelf supports.

A back panel made from ¼" plywood has a 1 × 3 nailing strip mounted 1½" below the top edge of the back panel and set in ⅜" on each side. It is fastened with glue and ¾" screws driven through the back panel.

How to Build & Install a Wall Cabinet

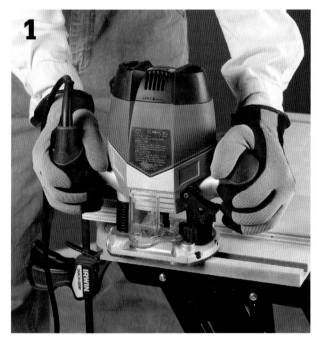

1

2

Measure and cut ¾" plywood side panels, then cut rabbets and dadoes using a router and a straightedge guide, following the dimensions in the project details (see page 60 and 61).

Drill two parallel rows of ¼"-diameter holes for pin-style shelf supports on the inside face of each side panel. Use a right-angle drill guide and a scrap of pegboard as a template to ensure that holes line up correctly. Holes should be no deeper than ⅜"—most right-angle drill guides include a depth stop.

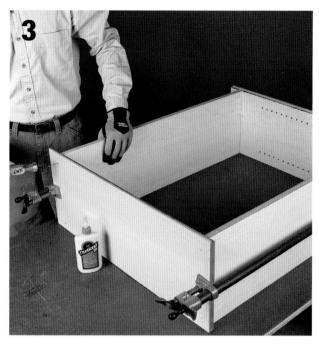

Measure and cut ¾" plywood top and bottom panels, then glue and clamp the side panels to the top and bottom panels to form the dado joints. Reinforce the joints with 2" finish nails driven every 3".

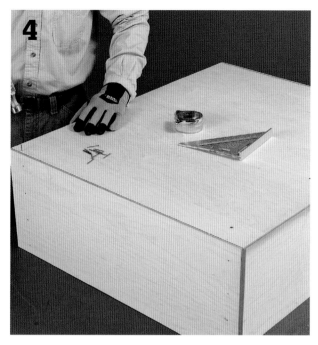

Attach the back panel (see pages 60 and 61) using glue and ¾" screws. Set the back panel into the rabbets at the back edges of the cabinet. Secure the back with 1½" finish nails driven into the cabinet edges.

Attach a 1 × 3 nailing strip on the inside of the cabinet, about 1½" down from the top. Drive three ¾" wood screws through the back panel and into the nailing strip, and then drive a pair of 2" finish nails through the side panel and into the ends of the nailing strip.

Measure the height and width of the cabinet interior and then cut 1 × 3 face-frame rails that are 4 ¾" shorter than the cabinet width. Cut face-frame stiles 4" longer than the height. Glue, square, and then clamp the rails between the stiles. You could use biscuits, splines, or dowels to reinforce the joints (these need to be installed before clamping). Here, pocket screws are being driven at the joints of the face frame using a pocket screw jig.

(continued)

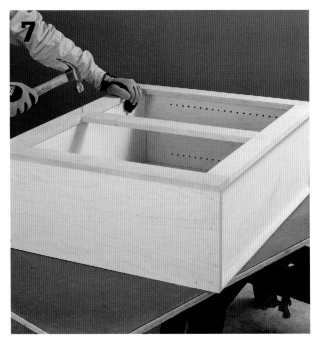

Center the face frame on the cabinet so the slight overhang on each side is equal, and the top edge of the bottom rail is flush with the bottom shelf surface. Attach the face frame with glue and 2" finish nails driven through pilot holes.

Use tinted wood putty that matches the color of the stained wood to fill nail holes. Sand all wood surfaces, and then apply wood stain (if desired) and two or three thin coats of polyurethane or other topcoat material.

Mark a level reference line on the wall where the bottom edge of the cabinet will be located—54" above the floor is a standard height. Locate the wall studs and mark their locations beneath the reference line.

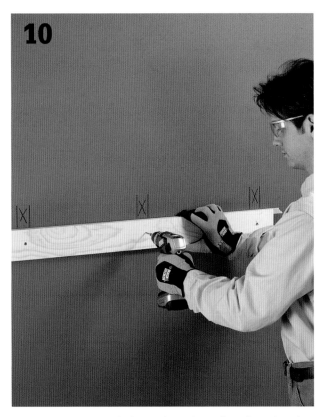

Screw a temporary ledger strip to the wall studs so that the top edge is flush with the reference line.

11

Install the cabinet by setting it onto the temporary ledger, and then brace it in position with a 2 × 4 wedged between the cabinet and the floor below (or the base cabinet, if present). Drill countersunk pilot holes in the nailing strip at the top of the cabinet, and drive 3" screws into the wall studs.

12

Use a level to make sure the cabinet is plumb. If not, loosen the screws slightly and insert shims behind the cabinet to adjust it to plumb. Tighten the screws completely, score the shims with a utility knife, and break off any excess.

13

Build or buy cabinet doors. A simple overlay door can be made from ½" plywood that matches the cabinet and door-edge molding that is mitered at the corners to frame the plywood panel. Hang the cabinet doors with hinges.

14

Build and install shelves. Here, shelves are made from ¾"-thick plywood with a ¼ × ¾" hardwood strip nosing on the front edge. Set the finished shelves on shelf pins inserted in the pinholes drilled in the cabinet side.

Base Cabinet Project Details

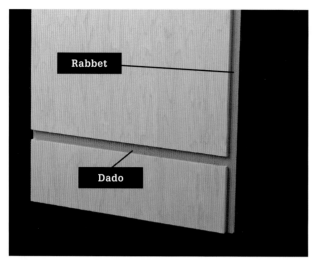

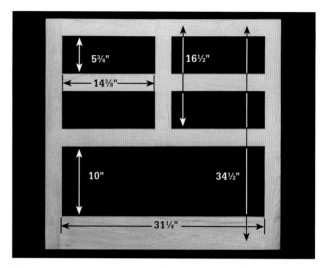

Side panels made from ¾" plywood have ¾"-wide, ⅜"-deep dadoes to hold the bottom panel, and ½"-wide, ⅜"-deep rabbets where the back panel will fit. The bottom dado is raised so the bottom drawer will be at a comfortable height.

The face frame includes 1 × 6 bottom rails and 1 × 3s for the stiles and other rails. Cut and assemble the face frame, following the dimensions shown in the photo above. Use biscuits, splines, or dowels to reinforce the joints. Alternately, drive pocket screws after the parts are glued and clamped.

How to Build & Install a Base Cabinet

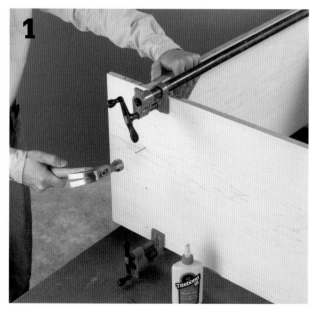

Cut the side and bottom panels from ¾" plywood (cabinet-grade maple is used here), and cut the ½" plywood back panel. Use a router and piloted rabbet bit to create ⅜ × ½" rabbets in the side panels for the back panel. Cut dadoes for the bottom panel into the side panels using a router, straight bit, and straightedge guide. Install the bottom panel between the side panels. Glue, clamp, and then drive finish nails through the side panels and into the ends of the bottom panel.

Install two 1 × 3 spreaders between the side panels at the top of the cabinet. Clamp the spreaders in position and attach them with glue and 2" finish nails driven through the side panels.

Build the face frame from 1 × 3 maple (actual sizes ¾ × 2½" and ¾ × 5¼"). The glued joints can be reinforced with biscuits, splines, or dowels prior to assembly, or they can be glued, clamped, and reinforced with pocket screws, as seen here.

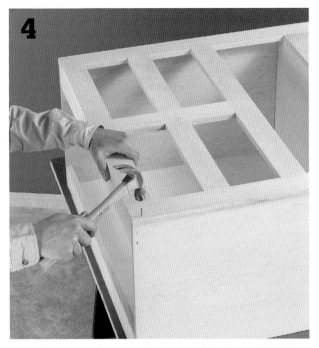

Attach the face frame to the cabinet with glue and 2" finish nails driven through pilot holes. The face-frame should be flush with the cabinet tops, slightly above the cabinet bottoms, and overhanging the sides equally by a small amount. Sand and finish the cabinet as desired.

Install the cabinet. Mark the locations of the wall studs in the project area, and then set the cabinet in place. Check with a level and shim under the cabinet, if necessary, to level it. Toenail the side panels to the floor at shim locations using 2" finish nails. Score the shims, and break off any excess.

Anchor the cabinet by driving 3½" screws through the back panel and into wall studs just below the top of the cabinet.

(continued)

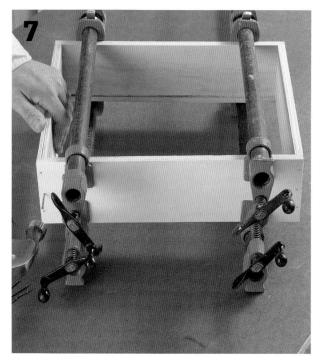

Build or purchase drawers. Simple overlay drawers are easy to make from ½" plywood and a false front made of hardwood. Refer to the information on page 69 for construction details and guidance on sizing drawers.

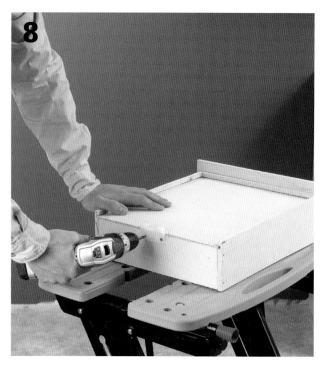

Install drawer slide hardware on the drawer. Slides may be center-mounted, as seen here, or side-mounted in pairs. Typically, side-mounted slides are rated for higher weight capacity.

Mount drawer slide hardware in the cabinet interior according to the manufacturer's instructions. Install the drawers and test the fit. Add drawer pull hardware.

Add the countertop of your choice. See pages 162 to 167 for information on choosing a countertop type and building it yourself. If you are building just a single base cabinet, consider a higher end material such as granite. The small scale will let you introduce an expensive material without spending a fortune.

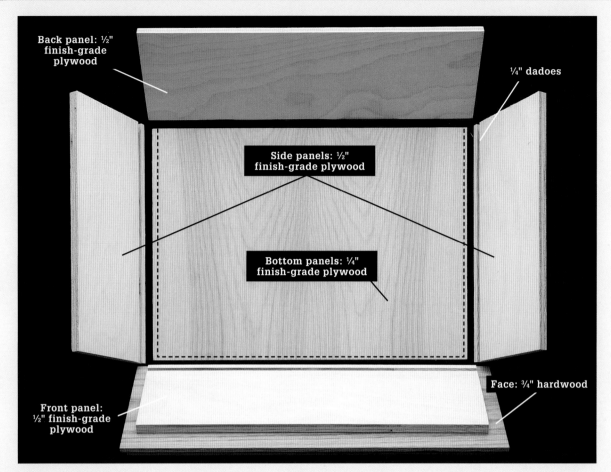

Back panel: ½" finish-grade plywood

¼" dadoes

Side panels: ½" finish-grade plywood

Bottom panels: ¼" finish-grade plywood

Face: ¾" hardwood

Front panel: ½" finish-grade plywood

Anatomy of an overlay drawer: The basic drawer box is made using ½" plywood for the front, back, and side panels, with a ¼" plywood bottom panel. The bottom panel fits into ¼" dadoes cut near the bottom of the front and side panels, and is nailed to the bottom edge of the back panel. The hardwood drawer face is screwed to drawer front from the inside, and it is sized to overhang the face frame by ½" on all sides. **Note:** This drawer is designed to be mounted with a center-mount drawer slide attached to the bottom of the drawer. If you use different hardware, like side-mounted drawer slides, you will need to alter this design according to the slide manufacturer's directions.

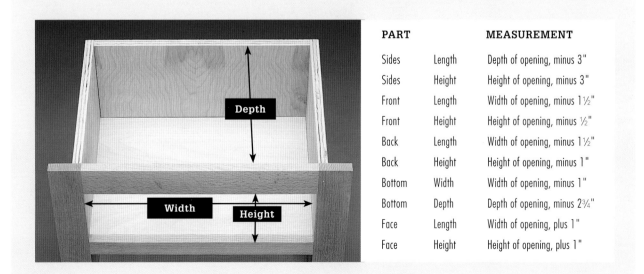

Depth

Width

Height

PART		MEASUREMENT
Sides	Length	Depth of opening, minus 3"
Sides	Height	Height of opening, minus 3"
Front	Length	Width of opening, minus 1½"
Front	Height	Height of opening, minus ½"
Back	Length	Width of opening, minus 1½"
Back	Height	Height of opening, minus 1"
Bottom	Width	Width of opening, minus 1"
Bottom	Depth	Depth of opening, minus 2¾"
Face	Length	Width of opening, plus 1"
Face	Height	Height of opening, plus 1"

Advanced Cabinet Projects

Building custom cabinets from scratch may seem daunting, but the construction process is actually simpler than you might think. You'll need some proficiency with a table saw and router, but the rest of the process is mostly gluing, clamping, and fastening the pieces together—all very manageable and straightforward skills for a proficient do-it-yourselfer. On the following pages, we provide the measured drawings and material lists to build an upper and base cabinet in the style shown for this contemporary kitchen. The design is clean and utilitarian but still very inviting, borrowing from both Shaker and Arts & Crafts influences. Best of all, these cabinets resonate quality and custom construction but are still quite easy to make. There's no panel-raising or cope-and-stick joinery to tackle when building the doors, and you won't even need to install crown moldings with complicated compound cuts to finish them off at the ceiling. Moldings are kept to a minimum here.

The upper cabinet doors feature a divided "field area," where you have the option to fill the frame with a plywood panel, glass panes, or a combination of both, depending on your preference. These doors overlay a face frame on the cabinet carcasses—a common style these days—and they are hung on adjustable, Euro-style cup hinges. The base cabinet doors use the same construction process as the upper cabinets, but they're even easier to make with a single plywood panel inside a four-piece frame. Drawer faces overlay the base cabinet face frames for easier installation, and they'll hide any minor irregularities that might occur when hanging the drawer boxes.

Obviously, these two plans will not cover the gamut of cabinet sizes your kitchen is likely to require, but they do provide a good starting point. And, you can use the same construction procedure to make cabinets and doors of different sizes by revising the material lists. Plan your kitchen cabinet project carefully. It's best to build each cabinet as a separate component, but always think in terms of uniformity when sizing the parts: your cabinets need to come together into a unified whole that looks intentional, while providing functional storage space for a home's busiest room. Also, be sure to follow the general guidelines provided on pages 30–31 to 88 for determining the heights and depths of cabinet carcasses and drawers. This will help you get the most from your building materials while meeting industry standards for accessibility and counter workspace.

Advanced Upper Cabinets

Building an upper cabinet will set a benchmark for how to build the rest of the cabinets in your kitchen, home office, workshop, or wherever you need them. The cabinet carcass, made of veneered plywood here, is typically joined at the four corners by rabbets reinforced with glue and screws. A wooden face frame covers the front of the carcass to hide the plywood edges and give the cabinet a finished look. Door-building happens next, followed by shelf construction so you can size the shelves to suit the "box" you've made. We'll step out the procedure here, building a double-door example measuring 34 inches wide and 30 inches tall — common proportions for a larger upper cabinet.

Tools & Materials ▸

Circular saw	Chisels
Table saw	Ear and eye
Jointer/planer	protection
Router table	(1) ¾" × 4 × 8 ft.
Drill/driver	maple plywood
Drill press	(1) ¼" × 4 × 4 ft.
Brad nailer or crown	maple plywood
stapler	¾" maple lumber
Combination square	Wood glue
Pocket hole jig	#8 × 1½" flathead
Shelf pin jig	wood screws
Dado blade	1¼" pocket screws
35mm Forstner bit	(4) Half overlay
Countersink bit	Euro-style hinges
Piloted rabbeting bit	⅛" tempered glass
Clamps	Shelf pins

If you have the proper woodworking and fabrication skills (and the time, tools, and energy), handsome, neat, and trim wall-mounted cabinets such as these may well be within your reach at a fraction of the cost of purchased custom cabinetry.

Cutting List

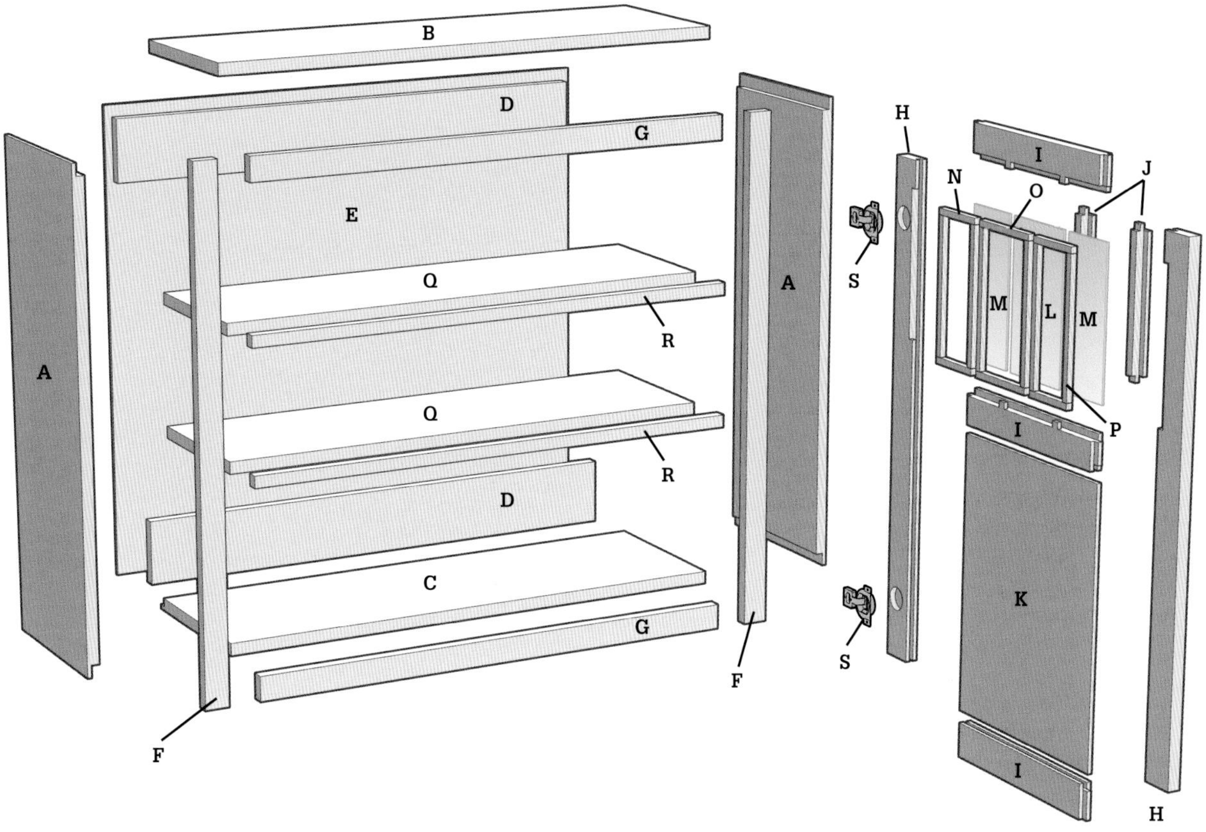

KEY	NO.	DESCRIPTION	DIMENSIONS	MATERIAL
A	2	Sides	¾ x 11¼ x 30"	Plywood
B	1	Top	¾ x 10¾ x 33"	Plywood
C	1	Bottom	¾ x 11¼ x 33"	Plywood
D	2	Back Rails	¾ x 4 x 32"	Plywood
E	1	Back	¼ x 33 x 29¾"	Plywood
F	2	Face-Frame Stiles	¾ x 1½ x 31½"	Maple
G	2	Face-Frame Rails	¾ x 1½ x 31"	Maple
H	4	Door Frame Stiles	¾ x 2 x 29½"	Maple
I	6	Door Frame Rails	¾ x 2 x 12¾"	Maple
J	4	Glass Muntins	¾ x 1¼ x 8¾"	Maple

KEY	NO.	DESCRIPTION	DIMENSIONS	MATERIAL
K	2	Door Panels	¼ x 12¾ x 16¼"	Plywood
L	2	Glass, Large	⅛ x 4¾ x 8¾"	Tempered
M	4	Glass, Small	⅛ x 3½ x 8¾"	Tempered
N	8	Glass Retainer, Short	⅜ x ⅜ x 3½"	Maple
O	4	Glass Retainer, Med.	⅜ x ⅜ x 4¾"	Maple
P	12	Glass Retainer, Long	⅜ x ⅜ x 8"	Maple
Q	2	Shelves	¾ x 9¾ x 31¾"	Plywood
R	2	Shelf Edging	¾ x ¾ x 31¾"	Maple
S	4	Hinges	Euro-style, Half Overlay	

How to Build an Advanced Upper Cabinet

Follow your material list to carefully lay out as many of the cabinet carcass parts as possible on each sheet of plywood. Arrange the parts so you can cut the sheets down to size with full-length or full-width cuts first. Then, use a fine-tooth blade on a circular saw to minimize splintering, and use a clamped straightedge to guide your cuts. When possible, cut the parts slightly oversized, then reduce them to final dimensions on the table saw.

Mill rabbets into the edges of the side panels to house the upper cabinet's top, bottom, and back panels. You can use a stacked dado blade set in the table saw to make these cuts, or a large straight bit in the router table as shown here. Attach featherboards to the router table fence to help press workpieces down flat against the table during routing.

Lay out and drill two rows of shelf pin holes into each of the cabinet side panels. A shelf-pin drilling template, as shown here, can speed this process along and ensure consistent spacing. It comes with a spring-loaded drilling guide that centers the bit within the template openings.

While the side panels are still fully accessible, drill pocket hole recesses for attaching the cabinet's face frame. A pocket hole jig sets the steep drilling angle, and guides a stepped drill bit in boring these holes. You can attach the face frame with glue or brad nails instead.

Sand the cabinet panels starting with 120-grit sandpaper and working down to 180 grit sandpaper, using a random orbit sander. It's much easier to do this now than when the cabinet is assembled.

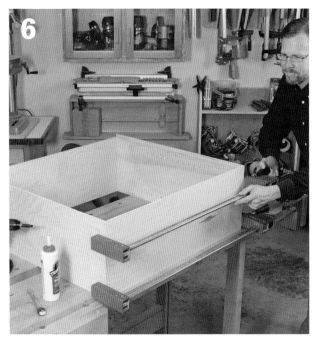

Assemble the cabinet parts without glue to make sure the joints fit together correctly. Disassemble and spread glue along the ends of the top, bottom, and side panels. Use bar or pipe clamps to hold the parts in place while the glue cures. Measure the diagonals and adjust the clamps if the measurements are not equal.

Drill countersunk pilot holes for the screws to keep the plywood from splitting and to recess the screw heads. For added strength, reinforce the corner rabbet joints by driving three or four #8 x 1 ½" flathead wood screws through the side panels and into the top and bottom panels.

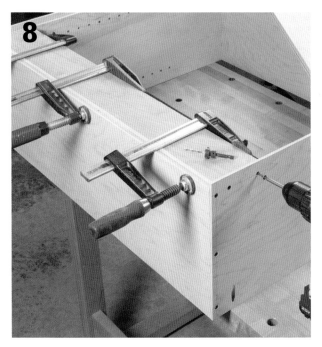

The upper cabinet's back rails help to square the carcass and provide attachment points for screws when hanging the cabinet on the wall. Cut these two rails to shape, and clamp them to the top and bottom panels. Align the rails flush with the bottoms of the back panel rabbets. Drive countersunk screws through the side panels to secure the rails.

(continued)

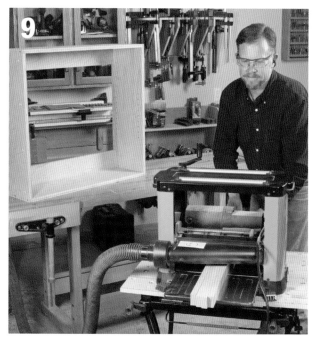

Prepare the face-frame rails and stiles from solid wood. If you start with flat, square stock, you can rip and crosscut these parts at your table saw. But a jointer and planer provides the advantage of removing minor warping or twisting before and after rough-cutting the parts to shape.

Lay out centered screw locations on the ends of the rails only. Clamp the face-frame rails vertically in the jig and bore the screw holes. A single 1 ¼" pocket screw will be sufficient for each joint.

Clamp the rails and stiles together on your worksurface, one joint at a time, before driving the attachment screws. A specialized "quick clamp" for pocket screws can make this process easier. It's unnecessary to drill a pilot hole in the stiles; the screws have self-piloting auger tips.

Cut the cabinet's back panel to size from ¼" plywood, and sand it with 180 grit. Apply two coats of a varnish or other wood finish to the inside surfaces of the cabinet carcass and the back panel. It's also a good idea to finish the outer surfaces to stabilize the plywood from moisture, even though most of these areas won't be visible after installation.

Fasten the back panel into its rabbets. You can use a pneumatic crown stapler (as shown here), brad nails, or short screws to attach the back. Drive fasteners every 6 to 8" around the panel's perimeter to hold it securely.

While the face frame could be installed with pocket screws alone, glue will reinforce these joints and keep the top and bottom panels aligned. Spread glue along the front edges of the cabinet carcass, and clamp the face frame in place. It will overhang the cabinet sides by ¼" and the bottom by ¾". Drive a 1 ¼" pocket screw into each hole.

Building Advanced Cabinet Doors

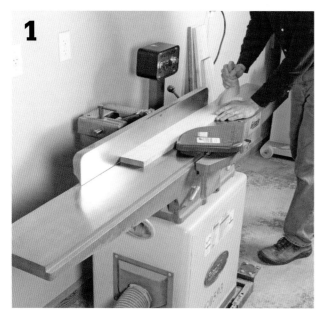

Use a jointer to remove minor distortions from door frame stock, and to help the doors stay flat once they're built and installed. If you don't have access to a jointer, buy the flattest boards you can find for your door frames.

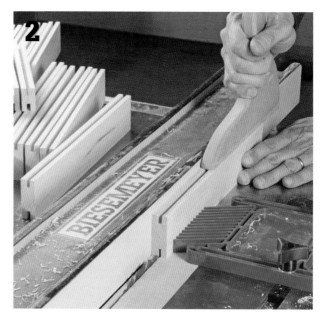

Rip and crosscut the door frame rails, stiles, and glass muntins to size. The drawer joinery begins with ¼"-wide, ³/₈"-deep grooves cut into one edge of the rails and stiles and into both edges of the intermediate door rail and the glass muntins. All the grooves can be milled at the table saw in two passes with a standard blade. Cut one half of the groove in one pass, then flip the piece end for end and cut the second half of the groove in a second pass.

(continued)

Cut centered tongues in the door rails and muntins by holding the workpieces vertically in a tenoning jig on the table saw, as shown. Use a dado blade. You can make the cuts with the same procedure, using a tenoning jig on the router table fitted with a straight bit.

Assemble the rails, stiles, and glass muntins without glue to check the fit of the tongue-and-groove joints. You may need to use a small hand plane or a file to pare down the tongues so that they fit better. The joints should slip together without force but not be overly loose.

Cut plywood door panels to fit the two large openings in the door frames; use the "dry-assembled" frames to determine the final proportions of these panels. Sand all of the door parts with 180 grit sandpaper, and mark the glass muntin locations on the top and intermediate rails with pencil lines. Spread glue on the frame joints and assemble the doors with the plywood panels in place. Clamp the doors until the glue cures.

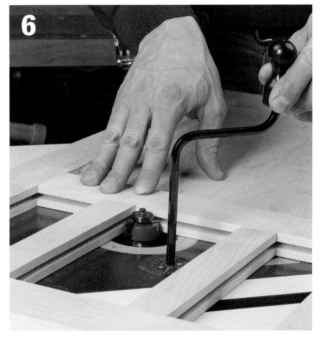

Glass panels will be fitted to the upper door frame openings by first removing the back wall of the grooved areas. Install a rabbeting bit in your router table, with a bearing on the bit that limits its cutting width to ³/₈". Raise the bit until the cutters will remove the entire back wall of material and the bearing will ride along the groove's front wall.

Rout the channel for the glass by feeding the door clockwise around the bit with the bearing riding along the inside edge of the glass openings. Press the doors down firmly against the router table as you proceed, and keep your hands well clear of the bit at all times.

Mark the inside corners for squaring with a pencil and square. Use a chisel and mallet to square the corners and create perfectly square, clean openings for the glass.

Measure the openings and have panes cut about $^{1}/_{16}$" small all around. Prepare long and short glass retaining strips from the same wood you used to make the frames. Install each pane with four retainer strips. Secure the glass with $^{1}/_{3}$" 18-gauge brads or 23-gauge pin nails, driving them horizontally through the retaining strips and into the frame.

Mark the location for the Euro-style cup hinges mounting holes in the doors, using the instructions that come with the hinges. Use a drill press with a 35mm Forstner bit. The doors should be clamped to the table and held firm against the fence.

Mark a line perpendicular to the layout line through the center of the cup hinge hole. Insert the hinges and align them with the lines. Use the screw opening on the hinges as references for drilling centered pilot holes for the mounting screws. (A self-centering vix bit makes this easy.) Fasten the hinges to the door.

Measure the hinge locations on the door frames, and transfer centered layout lines to the inside edges of the face frames to locate the cabinet-side hinge leaves. A commercially made jig, like the one shown here, makes it easy to locate the precise centerpoints for hinge leaf screws. Drill a pilot hole for each hinge screw with a self-centering Vix bit.

Attach the door hinges to the cabinet carcass, and test their action. Adjust the doors to hang evenly, relative to one another, and squarely over the face frame.

Cut the shelves for the cabinet. Cut ¾ x ¾" edging strips, a few inches longer than necessary. Mark the edging ¹/₁₆" wider than the shelf, so it will overhang the top and bottom. Spread glue on the contact surfaces and use long pieces of painter's tape to hold the edging in place.

When the glue cures, trim off the overhang with a piloted flush-trim bit. Set the bit depth so the bearing will ride along clean plywood. It may help to clamp both shelves together, as shown here, to provide a more stable surface for the router base. Trim the ends of the edging flush with the shelves to complete them.

Advanced Base Cabinets

In simplest terms, a base cabinet is really just a deeper and shorter version of an upper cabinet. When you build it, you'll follow almost the same construction process. In the following project, we'll make a standard 30"-wide base cabinet with a single drawer and double doors beneath. The overall height of this cabinet is 29¾" because it's intended to be set on a separate 4¾"-tall toe-kick plinth to raise it to the standard 34½" base cabinet height. (For more on this toe-kick style, see pages 44–46.) You'll notice that in the first photo of this series, the base cabinet carcass is already mostly assembled. Just follow the steps for building the upper cabinet, found on pages 72 to 80, and use the Base Cabinet Material List provided here. Aside from differences in part sizing, the only significant departure for building the carcass is that the top consists of two rails for attaching a countertop instead of a solid top panel. Build and hang the paneled doors, and make the shelves just as you would for the upper cabinet. What makes the base cabinet unique from the upper cabinet is drawer construction, and that's what we'll focus on here.

Tools & Materials ▸

Circular saw
Table saw
Jointer/planer
Router table
Drill/driver
Drill press
Brad nailer or crown
    stapler
Combination square
Pocket hole jig
Shelf pin jig
Dovetail jig and bit
Dado blade
35mm Forstner bit
Countersink bit
Clamps

Ear and eye
    protection
Maple plywood
    ¾" × 4 × 8 ft. (1)
Maple plywood
    ¼" × 4 × 4 ft. (1)
Maple lumber ¾"
Wood glue
Flathead wood
    screws
    #8 × 1½"
Pocket screws 1¼"
Half overlay Euro-
    style hinges (4)
Full-extension
    drawer slides 20"
Shelf pins

Take the time to ensure your base cabinets are perfectly level and you'll wind up with a simple and pleasing look like this.

Cutting List

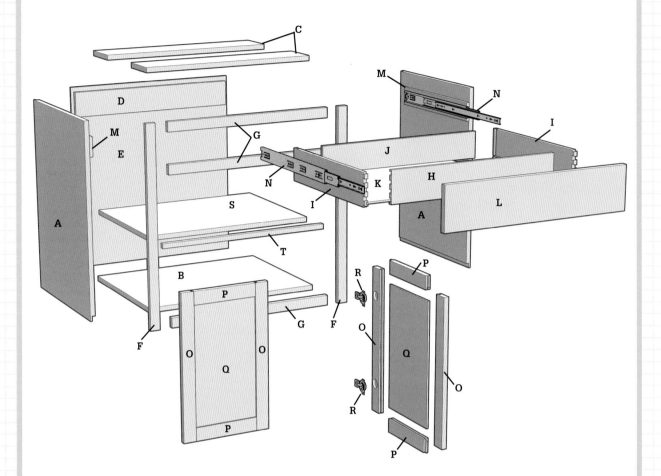

KEY	NO.	DESCRIPTION	DIMENSIONS	MATERIAL
A	2	Sides	¾ x 22½ x 29¾"	Plywood
B	1	Bottom	¾ x 22 x 29"	Plywood
C	2	Top Rails	¾ x 6 x 28"	Plywood
D	1	Back Rail	¾ x 4 x 28"	Plywood
E	1	Back	¼ x 29 x 29¾"	Plywood
F	2	Face-Frame Stiles	¾ x 1½ x 30½"	Maple
G	3	Face-Frame Rails	¾ x 1½ x 27"	Maple
H	1	Drawer Front	½ x 4½ x 26"	Maple
I	2	Drawer Sides	½ x 4½ x 20"	Maple
J	1	Drawer Back	½ x 3⅞ x 25½"	Maple

KEY	NO.	DESCRIPTION	DIMENSIONS	MATERIAL
K	1	Drawer Bottom	¼ x 19⅝ x 25⁷⁄₁₆"	Plywood
L	1	Drawer Face	¾ x 6 x 28"	Maple
M	2	Drawer Slide Spacers	½ x 3 x 20"	Maple
N	2	Drawer Slides	20" Full Extension	
O	4	Door Stiles	¾ x 2 x 22"	Maple
P	4	Door Rails	¾ x 2 x 10¾"	Maple
Q	2	Door Panels	¼ x 10¹¹⁄₁₆ x 18¹¹⁄₁₆"	Plywood
R	4	Hinges	Euro-style, Half Overlay	
S	1	Shelf	¾ x 21 x 27¾"	Plywood
T	1	Shelf Edging	¾ x ¾ x 27¾"	Maple

How to Build an Advanced Base Cabinet

Attach the sides, bottom panel, and top and back rails with glue and countersunk screws to form the base cabinet carcass. As with the upper cabinet, the bottom panel fits into a ¾ x ¾" rabbet in the side panels, and the back panel recesses into a ½ x ½" rabbet. Once the back is installed, follow the drawings and Material List to build a face frame for your base cabinet, and attach it to the front of the carcass with glue and pocket screws.

Attach a pair of ½"-thick wood spacers to the cabinet walls inside the drawer opening. Position these flush with the back of the face frame and so the drawer slides will be centered vertically on the drawer box. Then attach a drawer slide to each spacer with the short screws provided. The "cabinet side" slides should be flush with the front of the face frame when retracted.

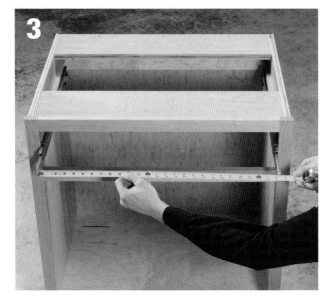

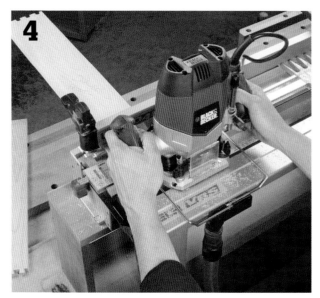

Clip the drawer side pieces of the drawer slides in place, and pull them out a few inches. Carefully measure the distance between them to determine the final length of the drawer front; depending on how accurately you've built the cabinet carcass, this distance may not match the drawer front dimension specified in the Material List. Regardless, the drawer needs to fit this space as accurately as possible for smooth action.

Cut the drawer front and sides to size. Here we're using a dovetail jig and plunge router to create half-blind dovetail joints. It's a classic and sturdy option for custom cabinet drawers. If you don't have a dovetail jig, you can assemble your drawer with rabbets, rabbet-and-dado joints, box joints, or even simple butt joints reinforced with glue and brad nails.

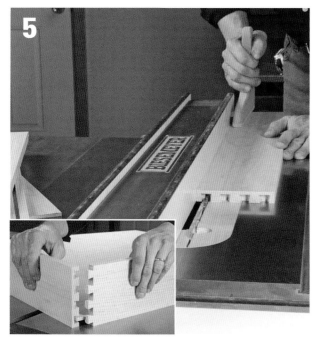

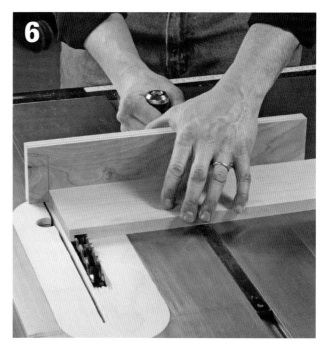

The drawer's ¼"-thick bottom panel fits into ¼"-deep grooves in the drawer front and sides. Position these grooves on your corner joints so that they will be hidden when the drawer box is assembled (see inset photo). Here, we're locating them ½" up from the bottom edges of the box parts. You can cut the grooves with a standard blade in two side-by-side passes, or with a ¼"-wide dado blade.

The drawer back fits between the drawer sides in ¼"-deep dadoes. Mill them ½" wide with a stacked dado blade in your table saw. Back the drawer sides up against a miter gauge to make these cuts safely and accurately. If you don't have a dado set, you can use a ½"-wide straight bit in a router table using the same technique.

Assemble the front, sides, and back panel with glue and clamps to form the drawer box; be sure the bottom edge of the drawer back is flush with the top edge of the drawer bottom grooves. When the glue cures, slide the drawer bottom into place, and fasten it to the drawer back with crown staples, brad nails, or short screws.

Sand the drawer box. Mark center lines along the length of the drawer sides to position the drawer side slide components. The instructions that come with the slides will suggest driving just a few screws at first into the slotted holes so you can make minor adjustments with the drawer hanging in the cabinet.

Cut the drawer face to size, and hang the drawer box in the cabinet. Pull it out a few inches and install two small clamps to keep it from closing. Use short strips of double-sided carpet tape, applied to the drawer box front, to hold the drawer face in place. Position it for an even overhang all around the drawer opening.

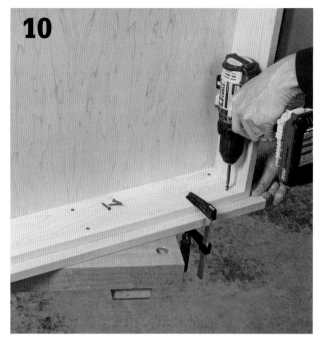

10

Clamp the drawer face and front together to keep these workpieces from shifting, and pull the drawer out of the cabinet. Drive several 1" countersunk screws through the drawer front and into the drawer face to secure them permanently. Re-hang the drawer.

11

Locate the center of the drawer face and clamp the handle drilling jig in place. Use a center punch or a scratch awl to poke points for the drawer pulls through the jig's holes. Drill the holes for the hardware through the drawer face and front.

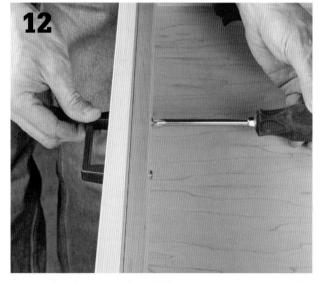

12

Attach the drawer pull by driving the screws that come with it through the drawer front and face. **Note:** you may need to purchase longer screws than come with the hardware. Or, as another option, you could drill deep counterbores through the drawer front to make use of the shorter screws.

13

Test the action of the drawer in its opening. If you are satisfied with the locations of the slides and the drawer sits evenly, drive more screws through the round holes in the slides to fix them permanently in place.

Building Drawers

Drawers, and especially hand-built drawers, used to be limited mostly to storing small items. But the development of very reliable and smooth-operating drawer slide hardware has made it possible for DIYers to build larger, custom drawers that function just as well as smaller drawers. For example, you can now choose to install a set of large drawers instead of doors in a base cabinet, eliminating the need to stoop and reach deep into the back of a base cabinet. This convenience has made it possible for an increasing number of homeowners to opt for drawers instead of doors when designing built-ins.

Modern mechanical drawer slides place less stress on drawer joints. As a result, the joinery required to build a drawer is less critical. It is not difficult to build a functional and durable drawer box.

It's most practical to build drawers that feature a separate drawer box and drawer face because the position of the drawer face can be adjusted to ensure a perfect final appearance. Make drawer fronts that match the rest of the cabinet. Solid-wood slab construction is a common type of drawer front because many drawers are too narrow for frame-and-panel construction. To build a frame-and-panel drawer front, the drawer box should be at least 7 inches tall.

Solid wood is most often used for drawer faces because the edge grain is exposed around the edge of the face. You can use plywood to make a drawer face, but you must attach solid or veneer edge banding if you want to cover the exposed plywood edges. Plywood is a good material for building the drawer boxes. It's very stable, eliminating most of the construction concerns about expanding or contracting wood parts. Use ½"-thick Baltic birch plywood for the sides and ¼"-thick plywood for the bottom. Substitute ½"-thick plywood for the bottom if the drawer is wider than 30" or if you have extra ½" plywood.

Building drawers from scratch is much easier to do if your shop is equipped with a set of good pipe clamps.

Drawer Face Styles

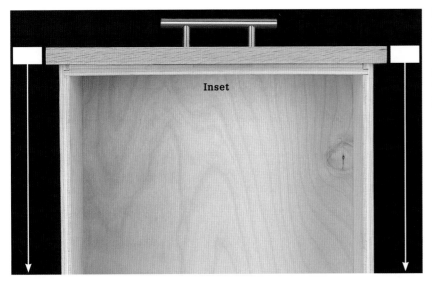

Inset drawer faces fit fully inside the face-frame or frameless cabinet opening with the front surfaces flush. Inset drawer faces are the trickiest type to install because they must fit perfectly inside the face frame or the uneven gap (called the reveal) around the face will show the error.

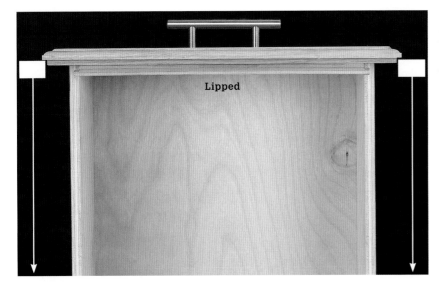

Lipped drawer faces have rabbets cut along the back edges to create a recess that fits over the face frame. The net effect is that the front surface of the drawer front will be ⅜" proud of the cabinet. Lipped drawers are not traditionally attached to a separate drawer box, but they can be.

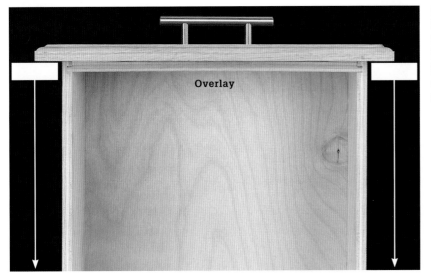

Overlay drawer faces close against the face frame. The front edges of the drawer front normally are profiled. Overlay drawer faces are the most common type used today because they are the easiest to make and install. Overlay faces are almost always used on frameless cabinets.

Determining Drawer Dimensions

You need to consider several factors when calculating drawer box dimensions; the type of cabinet, the size of the cabinet, the type of drawer face, and the type of drawer slides you plan to install.

The length of the drawer box is calculated as the distance from the front of the box to the back. Drawer boxes for standard (24"-deep) cabinets are typically 22" long. If the drawer face will be inset, then subtract ¾" for the drawer face. If the drawer face is lipped, then subtract the amount of drawer face that will be recessed into the face frame. If the drawer face is overlay, then the drawer box will be flush with the front of the cabinet. You must also leave space (typically 1") behind the drawer to ensure that it will close without hitting the back of the cabinet.

The width of the drawer box is the distance from the left outside edge of the box to the right outside edge. Measure the width of the drawer opening and subtract the required drawer slide clearance (see the manufacturer's installation instructions). Most drawer slides require ½" on each side of the box. For face

frame cabinets, measure the distance between the inside edges of the face-frame stiles. For frameless cabinets, measure the distance between the inside faces of the cabinet sides. Your width measurement must be precise because most drawer slides have very limited play for adjustment.

The depth or height of the drawer should leave at least ¼" clearance above and below the top and bottom edges of the drawer. For face-frame cabinets, measure the distance between the rails above and below the drawer opening. Then subtract at least ½" (¼ + ¼") for clearance above and below the drawer. For frameless cabinets you must lay out the number of drawers that will fill the cabinet and determine each drawer depth, including a ¼" clearance above, below and between each drawer.

Once you have calculated the overall dimensions you can cut the drawer parts to size. The dimensions of each part will depend on the type of joinery you use to construct your drawers.

Although this drawer and front were supplied by a custom manufacturer (you'll have a hard time replicating the interior organizers), the idea is simple and the same if you're building your own drawers: overlay drawers will be easier to create and look better in the end.

Face-Frame Cabinets

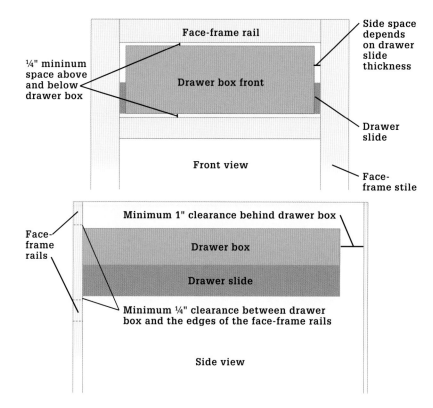

Face-frame rail

Drawer box front

Side space depends on drawer slide thickness

¼" mininum space above and below drawer box

Drawer slide

Front view

Face-frame stile

Face-frame rails

Minimum 1" clearance behind drawer box

Drawer box

Drawer slide

Minimum ¼" clearance between drawer box and the edges of the face-frame rails

Side view

Cabinets with face frames. When determining the required size for custom-built cabinet drawers, use the inside dimension of the face-frame opening as your guide. There should be a gap of at least ¼" (and not much more) at the top and bottom of the opening. The side-to-side measurement of the drawer should leave a gap of about ½" to create space for a side-mounted drawer slide. The illustration shown here is for the drawer box and should not affect false-front dimensions if your drawer will have one.

Frameless Cabinets

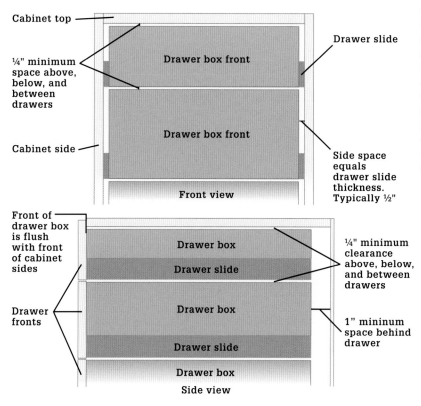

Cabinet top

Drawer box front

Drawer slide

¼" minimum space above, below, and between drawers

Drawer box front

Cabinet side

Side space equals drawer slide thickness. Typically ½"

Front view

Front of drawer box is flush with front of cabinet sides

Drawer box

Drawer slide

¼" minimum clearance above, below, and between drawers

Drawer box

Drawer slide

Drawer fronts

Drawer box

1" minimum space behind drawer

Side view

Cabinets without face frames. The clearances required for a drawer box in a frameless cabinet are pretty much the same as they are for framed cabinets. Laying out drawer slide locations can be a little trickier without face-frame rails to frame the top and bottom of each opening. The best way to manage this is to lay your cabinet sides next to each other with the tops and bottoms aligned, and then gang-mark the locations for the slides.

Butt-Joint Drawer Box Construction

A very simple, but effective, way to build drawers is to join the corners with butt joints and secure the bottom in grooves that are cut into the sides. You can build this type of drawer using a router table or table saw. Or you can use a circular saw and miter saw to cut the parts to size and a router to cut the grooves.

First calculate the part dimensions (see illustration, below). Then cut the parts to size. Next, cut the groove in the sides that will hold the bottom panel. Use a dado blade set or make multiple passes with a regular table saw blade to cut the groove wide enough to fit the drawer bottom.

Test the fit of the bottom panel. The bottom should fit snug in the groove and the tops should align. If it doesn't fit, then move the fence out slightly and make another pass to make the groove a little wider.

Assemble the drawer box with glue and brad nails. Apply a thin bead of glue to the inside of the grooves. Fit the bottom panel into the grooves. Then apply a bead of glue to the end edges and bottom edges of the front and back pieces. Next, slide the front and back pieces between the sides and attach them (photo 3). Carefully flip the drawer over. Adjust the drawer to be square and attach the bottom to the front and back (photo 4).

DRAWER BOX WITH BUTT JOINTS

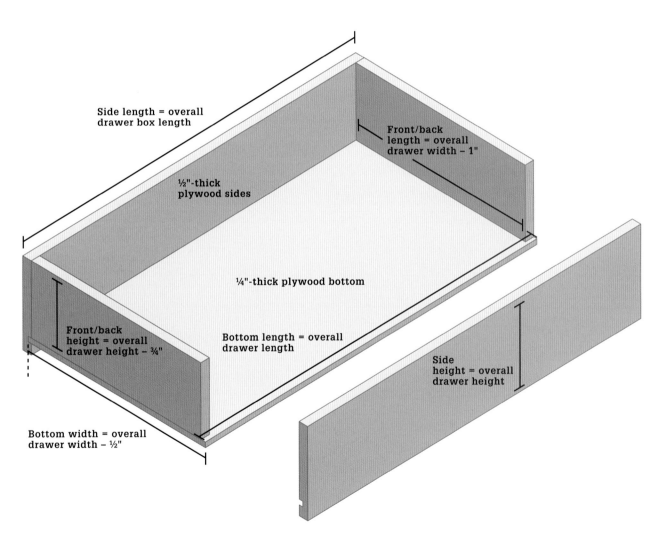

Side length = overall drawer box length

Front/back length = overall drawer width – 1"

½"-thick plywood sides

¼"-thick plywood bottom

Front/back height = overall drawer height – ¾"

Bottom length = overall drawer length

Side height = overall drawer height

Bottom width = overall drawer width – ½"

How to Construct a Butt-Joint Drawer Box

Cut the drawer parts to width on a table saw if you have one. Otherwise, use a circular saw and a straightedge cutting guide. Cut the parts to length with a power miter saw.

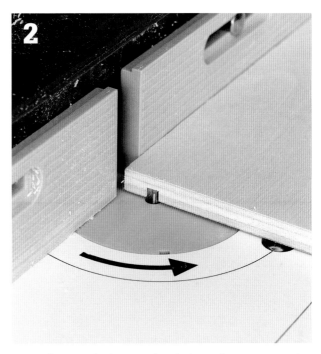

Cut a slot near the bottom of each drawer box part to create access for the drawer bottom, which usually is made from ¼" or ½"-thick plywood. The slot should be slightly wider than the thickness of the drawer bottom panel. You can cut it with a router, or on a table saw using multiple cutting passes.

Attach front and back to sides with 18 ga. × 1¼" brad nails. Hold the nail gun in line with the sides to reduce the chance of the nails curving and popping through the front or back pieces.

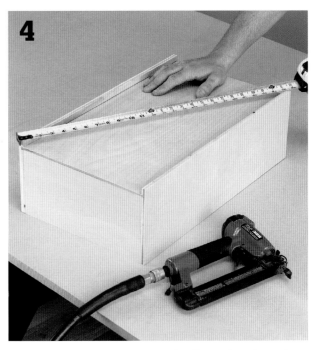

Use a square or measure across the diagonals to determine if the drawer sides are square to the front and back. Adjust the drawer to be square and attach the bottom to front and back with 18 ga. × 1" brad nails.

Rabbet-and-Dado Box Construction

The rabbet-and-dado joint is a more advanced and durable joint that is commonly used to build drawer boxes. There are several benefits that make the rabbet-and-dado joint a good choice for drawer box corner joints. It features multiple gluing surfaces. The tongue of the rabbet provides structural joint strength against the force of opening or closing the drawer. And,

although it's not as intricate as a dovetail joint, it is attractive and more decorative than a simple butt joint.

After the parts are cut to size, you can make the joints with a router table and ¼" straight bit. Or, you can follow the same construction process and make these joints with a table saw and ¼"-wide dado blade set.

RABBET-AND-DADO DRAWER BOX

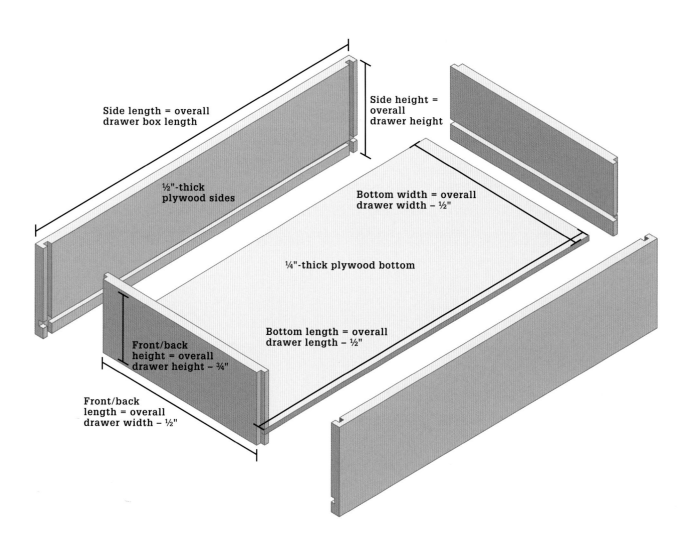

Side length = overall drawer box length

Side height = overall drawer height

½"-thick plywood sides

Bottom width = overall drawer width – ½"

¼"-thick plywood bottom

Front/back height = overall drawer height – ¾"

Bottom length = overall drawer length – ½"

Front/back length = overall drawer width – ½"

How to Make a Rabbet-and-Dado Box

Plywood Grades ▶

You'll find many grades of plywood when shopping for drawer box and cabinet case material. Plywood is graded A through D, with the letter designations describing the quality of the wood used in the outer plies, or faces. Plywood is also designated for interior or exterior use. The finish plywood used for drawer boxes should be grade B-B or better (A-A would indicate a high-quality, flaw-free exterior finish on both sides). We recommend Baltic birch plywood, produced from the Baltic nations. This is sheet plywood produced in both 5 x 5' and 4 x 8' sheets. Furniture grade interior Baltic birch plywood is knot- and streak-free, with an attractive appearance.

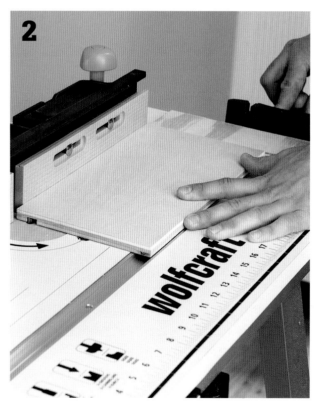

Place the drawer side face down on the router table and use a miter gauge to guide the piece through the cut. Cut a ¼ × ¼" dado located ¼" from each end of the inside face.

Cut the ¼"-wide × ¼"-deep grooves that will contain the bottom in the front, back, and side pieces. Set the fence ½" away from the edge of the bit. If you are using ½"-thick plywood for the bottom, make another pass to widen the grooves to ½". Test the fit of the drawer bottom in the groove. If the groove is too narrow, move the fence out slightly and make another pass to widen the groove.

(continued)

3 Cut the ¼ × ¼" rabbets in the ends of the front and back pieces. Place each piece face down and use a miter gauge to push it through the cut. Cut the rabbet in a scrap piece first, to check how well the rabbet fits in the drawer side-piece dado.

4 Bore ³⁄₁₆- or ¼"-dia. pilot holes through the drawer box front. Space the holes roughly 6" apart across the middle height of the drawer.

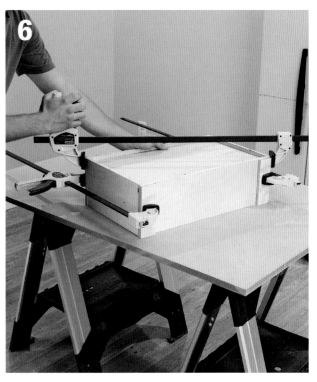

5 Dry-assemble the drawer box to make sure all the parts fit together well. When you're satisfied with the fit, assemble the drawer box with glue. Use cauls to apply even pressure across the joints.

6 Measure diagonally across the drawer to check for square. If the diagonal measurements are equal, then the drawer is square. If not, place a clamp across the longer diagonal and tighten the clamp to bring the drawer into square.

Installing Drawers

Drawers are mounted in the cabinet on drawer slides. There are many types of drawer slides, ranging from basic slides that cost only a couple dollars a pair, to very advanced motor-driven slides that can cost over $100 per pair. The two most common and versatile types of slides are roller slides and telescopic ball-bearing slides. Both types feature two basic components: a runner that attaches to the drawer and a guide that attaches to the cabinet.

It doesn't matter how beautifully constructed your drawers are; if the drawer slides aren't installed correctly, the drawer will not operate properly. The slides must be installed perpendicular to the cabinet face, level to each other, and the front edge of each slide must be the same distance from the front of the cabinet.

The slides are mounted directly to the sides of frameless cabinets. Face-frame cabinets require a spacer, cleat, or bracket to support the slide and keep it flush with the inside edge of the face frame.

It's easiest to mount the slides flush with the bottom of the drawer box. Place the box on a flat surface and attach the runners. Next, disconnect the guides from the runners. Attach the guides to the cabinet. Make a template to position the guides for each drawer at exactly the same height on both sides of the cabinet.

The front of the guide should be flush with the front of the cabinet or face frame when you are installing overlay drawer fronts. The front of the guide should be set back from the front when you are installing inset or lipped drawers. The setback distance equals the thickness of the face that is inset in the face frame. For example, if the drawer face on an inset drawer is ¾" thick, then the guide is installed ¾" back from the front of the face frame.

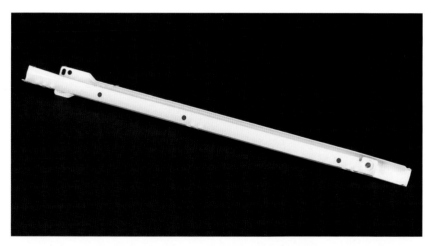

Roller slides are inexpensive and easy to install. The most common versions of these slides open 4" less than the length of the drawer.

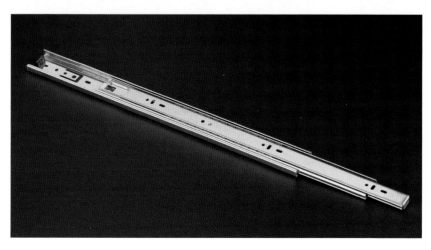

Telescopic ball-bearing slides are available in a wide range of sizes, providing weight-bearing and extension options to suit just about any application.

How to Install Drawer Slides

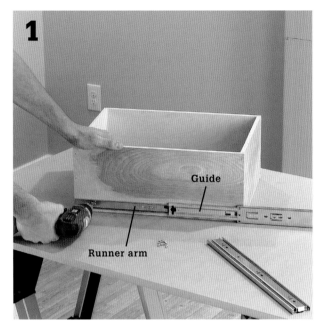

Place the drawer slide on a flat surface next to the drawer box. Extend the runner arm from the guide and align the front of the runner with the front of the drawer box. Drive screws into a couple of the slotted screw holes.

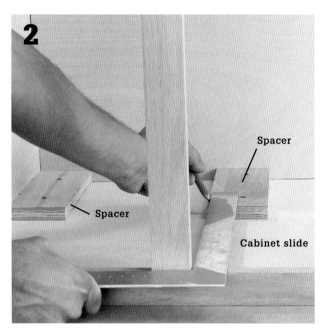

If your cabinet has face frames, make spacers that are the same thickness as the distance from the cabinet side to the inside edge of the face frame and attach them to the cabinet side. Use a framing square to mark a reference line on the spacers for each slide, level with the face-frame rail top.

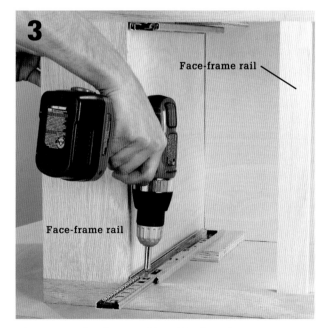

Disconnect the drawer slide guides from the runner arms that are mounted to the drawer box. Position the slides inside the cabinet drawer openings so the bottom edges are slightly above the face-frame rail and the other ends are flush with the reference lines marked on the spacer. Attach the guides to the cabinet by driving screws into the slotted screw holes.

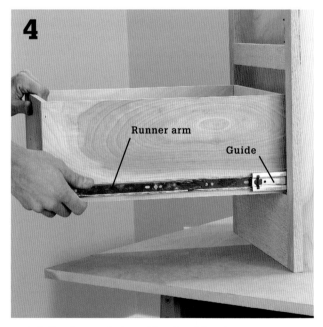

Install the drawer in the cabinet by sliding the runner arms back into the guides and snapping or locking them into place. Test the drawer operation and adjust the position of the runners and guides as necessary. Drive screws into the fixed screw holes once you are assured that the drawer operates properly.

Drawer Slide Spacer Options ▶

The drawer slides in a face-frame cabinet must be flush with the inside edge of the face frame. Mount the drawer slide guide to a spacer or bracket that is attached to the cabinet side or back.

Wood spacer

Back wall bracket

How to Adjust Drawer Slides: Box Is Too Narrow

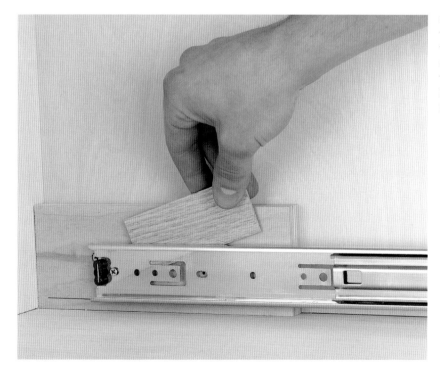

Cut enough shims to match the width that must be added to the drawer. Make the shims out of paper, cardboard, wood, or plastic laminate. Install shims between the slides and the cabinet side or spacer. Reinstall the drawer and test the fit. Add or remove shims until the drawer fits properly.

How to Adjust Drawer Slides: Box Is Too Wide

Sacrificial fence

Option 1: Attach a sacrificial fence to your table-saw fence. Lower the blade below the table. Move the edge of the fence over the blade. Turn on the saw and raise the blade up into the fence to the height of the drawer runner. Adjust the fence so that the width of the amount of blade that extends beyond the fence equals the amount you need to trim off the drawer. Make sure no fasteners are in the drawer in the cut area. Trim the drawer.

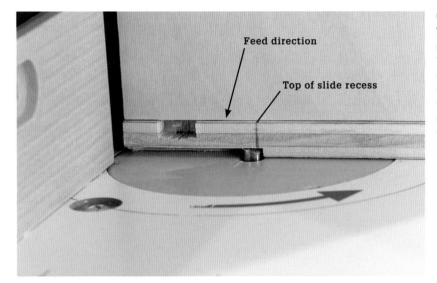

Feed direction

Top of slide recess

Option 2: Install a straight cutting bit in your router table. Set the fence so that the amount of the bit that extends above the table equals the amount you need to trim off the drawer. Set the fence so your first cut will be at the bottom of the recess for the slide. Move the fence back after each cut and continue cutting until you reach the top of the slide recess.

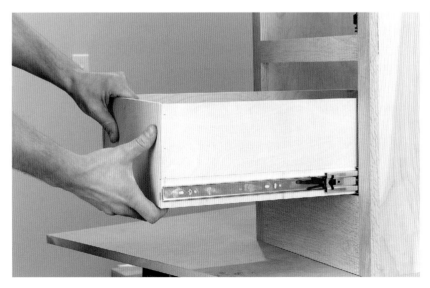

Reattach the runner arm and test the fit of the drawer. If the drawer is still too wide, then move the fence over slightly and trim a little more off the drawer side.

Attaching the Drawer Face

Finish the drawer face before you attach it to the drawer box. Carefully position the drawer face before you drive any screws. Inset drawer faces are centered in the face-frame drawer opening. Overlay drawer faces on frameless cabinets are centered over the cabinet sides. Drill screw starter holes in the back of the drawer face and attach the face with screws that will extend approximately halfway through the face. For example, use 1" long screws to attach a ¾"-thick face to a ½"-thick drawer box front.

Finally, attach the drawer knobs or pulls. If you are installing several drawers, use a jig to consistently bore the knob or pull pilot holes in the same place on every drawer face. The screws that are included with many knobs and pulls are intended for use on ¾"-thick material. You may have to purchase longer hardware screws to attach the knobs to a two-piece drawer face.

A drawer face made of solid hardwood gives the drawer a presentable appearance while maintaining the economy and strength of a plywood drawer box.

How to Attach the Drawer Face

Apply double-sided carpet tape or thin adhesive pads to the drawer front to temporarily attach the drawer face. Press the drawer face against the tape, using paper or cardboard spacers to help center drawer faces in face-frame openings as necessary.

Carefully slide out the drawers and attach the faces with No. 8 × 1" washer-head screws or panhead screws and washers. Drive the screws through pilot holes in the drawer box front.

Use a marking jig to mark drilling points for the drawer hardware pilot holes in the fronts of the drawer faces. Bore a ³⁄₁₆"-dia. pilot hole for each hardware screw. Attach the drawer pulls and install the drawers.

Building Cabinet Doors

If you don't want everything you've got stuffed in your cabinet to be on constant display, then you'll need to build some doors. Doors conceal and help keep dust off the cabinet contents. Doors also act as the face of the cabinet, defining the cabinet style.

There are many types of door construction, but the two most common are slab doors and frame-and-panel doors. Both types can be modified using different wood species, edge profiles, and finishes to create a style to fit just about any décor.

In addition to choosing the door style, you must also decide how the doors will be mounted on the cabinet. There are three main types of door mounts: inset, overlay, and lipped.

Tools & Materials ▸

- Ear and eye protection
- Work gloves
- Table saw
- Router table
- Power drill
- Combination square
- Belt and random orbit sanders

- 36" and 24" pipe or bar clamps
- Small hand saw (a Japanese pull saw is a good choice)
- Brad pusher
- Standard magnetic door catch

- Magnetic touch door catch (round piston style)
- Rail and stile router bit set
- Piloted rabbeting bit
- Concealed hinge jig system

- Self-centering drill bits (for drilling pilot holes with jigs)
- Wrap-around hinges
- Frameless overlay hinges
- Soft close hinge and cabinet adapters

Building your own cabinet doors lets you customize the design so you can have precisely the door type you want, such as these framed doors that are being fitted with glass panel inserts.

Common Cabinet Door Styles

A slab door is a flat panel. These doors can be made from solid stock, but they are most often constructed with a plywood panel that has its edges concealed with wood edging.

Frame-and-panel doors are the most popular door style. These feature a panel that is framed by two vertical stiles and two horizontal rails.

Door Mount Options

Overlay doors are most often mounted on frameless cabinets with concealed hinges, but these versatile doors can also be installed over a face-frame cabinet. They are more forgiving to install than inset doors because there is no exposed gap between the door and cabinet.

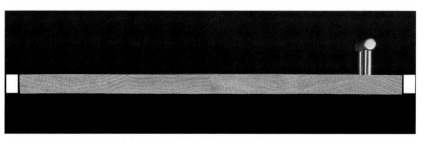

Inset doors are usually mounted on face-frame cabinets. The face of an inset door is flush with the face frame. These are the most challenging doors to install because they must be perfectly centered in the frame opening to maintain an even gap around the door.

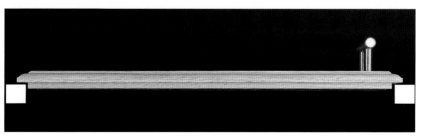

Lipped doors are a hybrid between inset and overlay. They feature a rabbet that is cut in the back edge to fit inside the face-frame opening. Lipped doors are often used on manufactured face-frame cabinets.

Determining Cabinet Door Sizes

The first step in building doors is to determine the size of the doors. To prevent sagging, the maximum width of each door should not be more than 24". If the cabinet opening is greater than 24" wide, use two doors.

If you are building large frame-and-panel doors or glass doors, design the doors with a bottom rail that is wider than the top rail. A wider bottom rail gives the door good proportions by adding a little more visual weight to the bottom of the door. A wider bottom rail also adds more gluing surface, creating a stronger frame to support the weight of the door.

Measuring for Cabinet Door Dimensions

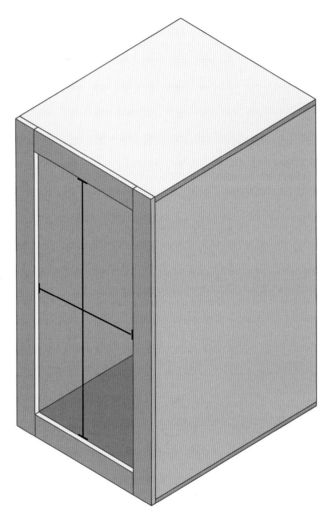

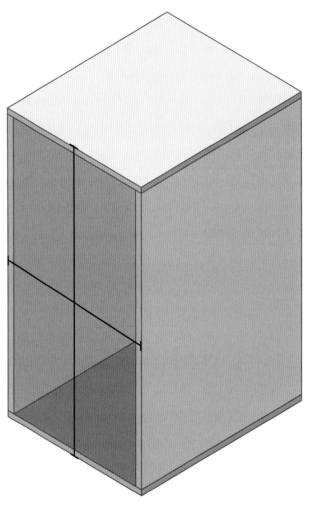

If you're installing inset doors, measure the height and width of the face-frame openings. Determine the door width and height by subtracting the width of the gaps that must be left around the edges of the doors and between doors.

If you are installing overlay doors, measure the height and width of the cabinet to the outside edges of the cabinet sides, top, and bottom. Then subtract ⅛" from the height and width measurements.

Building Frame-and-Panel Cabinet Doors

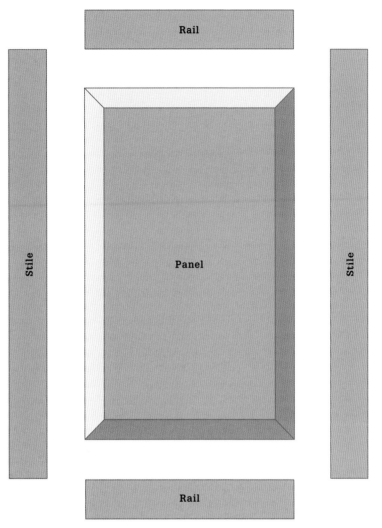

There are several ways to build frame-and-panel doors. The doors for this cabinet are made using a rail-and-stile, also referred to as a cope-and-stick, router bit set. This set contains two router bits; one bit that cuts the stub tenon in the ends of the rails, and a second bit that cuts the panel groove and edge profile.

Frame-and-Panel Router Bit Set ›

One of the most efficient ways to make a frame-and-panel door is with a router table and bit set often called a cope-and-stick bit set. The two bits in this set cut opposite profiles that fit together to create a tight corner joint. The coping bit (sometimes referred to as the rail cutter) cuts the stub tenons in the ends of the rails. The sticking bit (sometimes referred to as the stile cutter) cuts the groove and top-edge profile in the inside edges of the rails and stiles. There are also single combination router bits that make both the cuts by adjusting the bit height.

How to Build a Frame-and-Panel Door

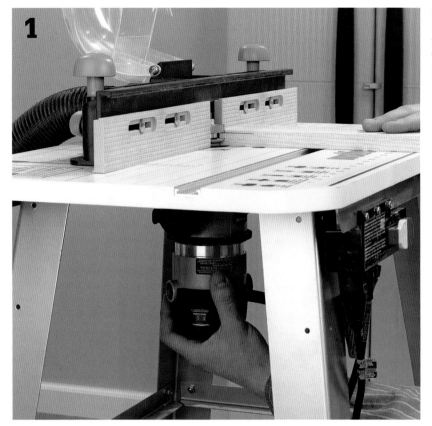

Set the bit height so that the bit will leave an ⅛"-deep rabbet above the stub tenon. Set the fence so that it lines up with the outside edge of the router bit pilot bearing.

Make test cuts in the ends of scrap pieces to check the bit height setting. Then cut the stub tenons in the ends of the actual rails, using a miter gauge to feed the rails face down past the bit. Be careful when routing small pieces like this; move slowly and steadily.

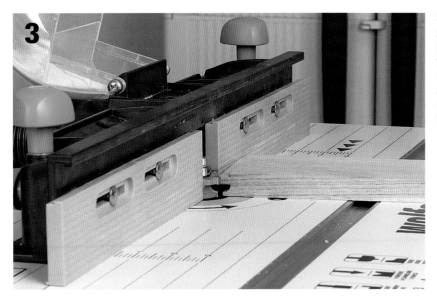

3

Set the sticking bit height so that the groove-cutting blade is aligned with the stub tenon on the rails. Set the fence so that it lines up with the outside edge of the router bit pilot bearing. Make test cuts in a scrap piece and adjust the bit height as necessary to create a perfect alignment between the rail and stile pieces.

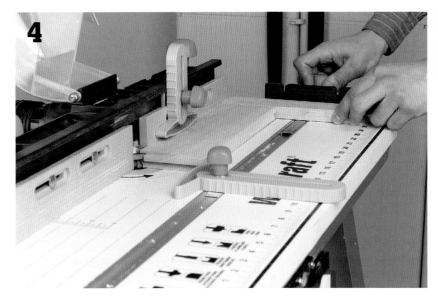

4

Feed the rails and stiles face down past the bit to cut the grooves in the inside edges of the stiles and rails. Use feather boards to help maintain even pressure throughout the cut.

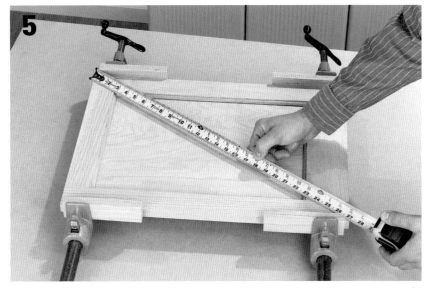

5

Dry-assemble the frame and measure the panel opening width and height. Cut the panel to size and sand it smooth. Apply finish to the frame parts and panel. Apply glue to the stub tenon joints, insert the panel in the grooves, and assemble the door frame. Clamp the frames. Measure across the diagonals to check the doors for square. If the measurements are equal, then the doors are square. If the measurements aren't equal, clamp across the longer diagonal to square the door.

Glass Panel Doors

Glass panel doors are a great way to equip a cabinet to highlight a favorite collection, beautiful glasses, or special occasion dinnerware. It's not much more difficult to install glass panels than it is to install solid insert panels made from plywood or another wood product. If you're installing real glass panels, it's always safest to purchase tempered glass for any door application. If you don't mind the look, you can also use clear acrylic or polycarbonate panels. These won't shatter, of course, but they tend to get scratched and will become cloudy over time.

Make and join the door frame rails and stiles the same way you'd do it for a plywood panel door (see pages 104-105), but assemble the frames without the panel and then install the glass panes in recesses you cut into the completed frames. If you have the capability and equipment, use mortise-and-tenon joints for the frame. The back inside edges of the frame opening must be rabbeted to create a recess against which the glass will fit.

Glass Cabinet Insert Options ▶

Although tempered glass is your safest and best choice for high-traffic cabinets that will be opened and closed every day, if you're building cabinets that will see less use, you might consider a more decorative glass for the opening. You can use "machined glass" inserts for an interesting effect that won't add much to the cost of the panes. Machined glass comes in uniform, repetitive textures, such as dimples and straight-line striations, and more random, irregular patterns such as "reamy" or "waterglass." Spend a little bit more and you can choose from a broad palette of stained-glass colors. Use them as a single sheet insert, or go a little more complex and lead different colors into the same cabinet door. You can also turn to other glass art forms for a totally unique look, such as sandblasted, painted, or even fused glass panels.

When considering glass inserts, you can pick from a lot more options than plain clear glass. The pebbled machine glass shown in these cabinets is just one of a wide range of textures available. You can also choose stained glass if you want to introduce a bit of color.

How to Make Glass Panel Cabinet Doors

Create the panel recess. First, install a ⅜"-dia. bottom-bearing rabbetting bit in your router. Secure the assembled wood frame to your work surface. Engage the router and cut a ⅜ × ⅜" recess around the entire back inside edge of the frame opening. Make these rabbet cuts in multiple passes of increasing depth.

Finish the cuts by using a wood chisel to square the corners. Remove the waste wood a little at a time, taking care not to split the wood or damage the corner joints.

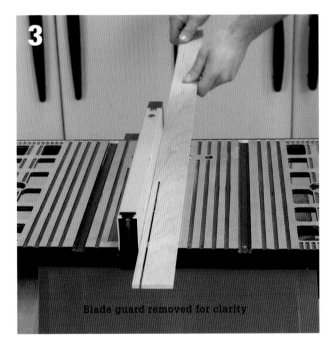

Blade guard removed for clarity

On a table saw, rip-cut wood stock (the same type used for the frame) into ¼ × ¼" lengths and then cut them to fit inside the frame opening, creating retainer strips. Use a push stick to move the narrow pieces across the blade. Sand and finish the doors and retainer strips to match the cabinet.

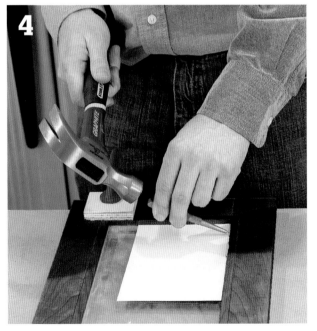

Cut the glass pieces (or have them cut) ⅛" shorter than the rabbeted frame opening in each direction. Cut the retainer strips to fit along each side of the glass. Bore ¹⁄₃₂"-dia. pilot holes through the retainer strips, spaced 6 to 8" apart, making sure the pilot holes are positioned so the brads will not contact the glass panel. Use a brad pusher or small tack hammer to drive ¾"-long brad nails through pilot holes and into the vertical surfaces of the frame recess opening. Then, set the nail heads with a nailset. **Tip:** Set a piece of cardboard over the glass surface to protect it.

Building Slab Doors

Slab doors are flat wood (as opposed to frame-and-panel doors). You can make them from a single piece of wood stock if you can find one wide enough, but this is usually not going to be possible. More often, slab doors are crafted by edge-gluing multiple strips of solid wood, or by attaching edging to a plywood panel. Plywood is used to make most slab doors because it is much more dimensionally stable than solid wood, and thus less likely to cup or warp.

The edges of plywood slab doors should be concealed with solid wood edging. If the doors will be used infrequently, iron-on veneer edge tape may be an acceptable way to cover the plywood edges.

The key to making a basic slab door is precise measurements. If the door is out of square even a minute amount, the error will be glaringly apparent as soon as it is mounted on the cabinet. You can cut a single piece of wood for the door, but this is not only expensive, it's often difficult to find lumber in the appropriate dimensions and in the species you prefer. The method shown here is actually less expensive and easier and, when done correctly, every bit as stable and sturdy.

Tools & Materials ▸

Table saw or circular saw with straightedge
Hand saw
Masking tape
¾" cabinet-grade plywood
¼"-thick edging strips
Glue
Sandpaper
Eye and ear protection
Work gloves

To make plywood doors with ¼"-thick solid wood edging, first subtract ½" from the height and width of the finished door size. Cut the plywood to these dimensions. Use solid stock that is slightly thicker than the plywood to make the edge strips. This is pretty easy to do, since most of the veneered plywood that we refer to as ¾" thick is actually slightly smaller.

Tip ▸

Make your own edging strips instead of buying pre-milled molding. Rip-cut ¼"-thick edge strips from ¾" hardwood stock using a table saw. Use a push stick to feed the thin stock past the blade.

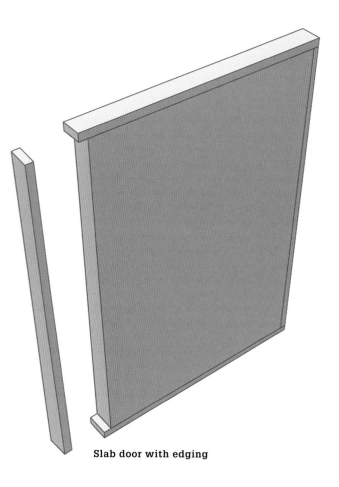

Slab door with edging

How to Make a Slab Door

Use a table saw or circular saw and straightedge guide to cut the plywood panels to size. Remember to allow for the edging strip thickness when determining the required panel size to yield a door that's the final dimensions you need.

Attach the side edging strips with glue. Stretch masking tape across the strips to hold them down tightly while the glue dries. Make sure none of the plywood edge is exposed beyond the edge pieces.

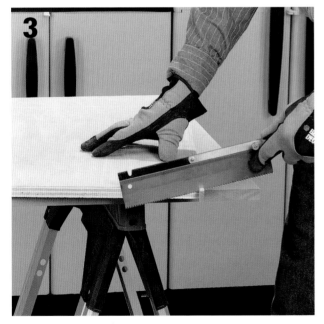

After the glue dries, remove the tape or clamps and use a hand saw (a gentleman's saw, back saw, or flush-cutting saw will do) to trim the ends of the edging flush. Touch up the cuts with sandpaper so that the strip ends are flush with, and square to, the panel.

Cut the top and bottom edging strips to length and secure them to the door edges with glue. Trim the ends of the edging strips once the glue has dried. Sand the edges of the edging strips so they are flush with both the back and front plywood faces. Use a sanding block and 150-grit sandpaper, and be careful not to sand through the veneer.

Hanging Cabinet Doors

Unlike others doors in your house, cabinet doors don't come pre-hung unless you buy stock cabinets. But luckily, mounting a cabinet door is a good deal simpler than hanging a house door directly into existing jambs with butt hinges. This is especially true since newer, easier-to-install hinge hardware has taken over most of the cabinetry market. The two most popular of the newer hinge types are concealed "cup" hinges and wrap-around butt hinges.

Concealed hinges are sometimes referred to as cup hinges because of the inset hinge cup component, and also as European hinges because, until recently they were primarily made by European hardware manufacturers. These hinges have been used for many years by professionals and commercial cabinet manufacturers, but they are now available at home centers for woodworking hobbyists and DIYers.

One of the biggest benefits of concealed hinges is their adjustability. Some models can be adjusted on all three planes: up/down, left/right, and in/out, making it much easier to achieve a perfect fit.

Concealed hinges feature two components: a hinge cup that recesses into the door, and a mounting plate that attaches to the side of the cabinet or to the face frame. Installing these hinges typically requires a 35mm Forstner drill bit. This type of bit bores the flat bottom hole into which the hinge cup sits. This hole is drilled with a drill press or a special right-angle drill guide. There are also specially designed concealed hinge jig kits that include the bit, right-angle guide, and positioning jig. These kits make installing this type of hinge very easy.

Follow the installation instructions included with most concealed hinges. The basic installation process is to first hold the door in position against the cabinet or face frame. Then mark the center location of the hinges on the door and cabinet side or face frame. Next, bore the hinge cup mortise. Then install the hinge cup component to the door. Fasten the mounting bracket to the cabinet side. Finally, mount the hinge arms on the mounting plates and adjust the door position.

Concealed cup hinge

Modern cabinet door hinges have two big advantages over simple butt hinges: they are faster to install and they are easier to adjust.

How to Install Concealed Hinges

1

Mark the center of the hinge location on the back of the door and cabinet side or face frame. Use a template to ensure that the hinge marks are exactly the same top and bottom.

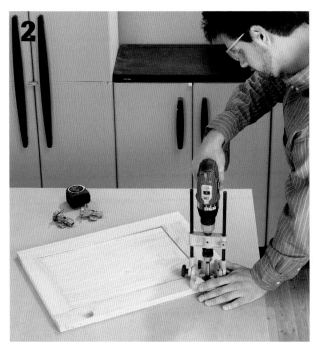

2

Use a drill guide and jig or a drill press to bore the cup mortise. This mortise dimension is typically 35mm dia. × 8-mm deep. Check your hinge installation directions for specific mortise dimensions.

3

Fasten the hinge-cup component to the door with the supplied hinge screws. Use a combination square to make sure the hinge arm is perpendicular to the door edge.

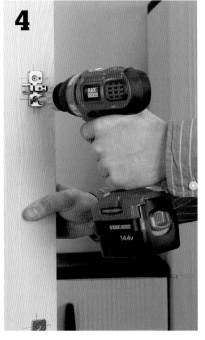

4

Follow the manufacturer instructions or use a jig to position the mounting plate on the hinge center mark that you made on the cabinet side.

5

Adjust the door position by loosening or turning the hinge adjustment screws.

Wrap-Around Butt Hinges

Butt hinges are the hardware of choice for many face-frame cabinets. Consider using a wrap-around butt hinge when you are hanging a heavy inset-door on a face frame. These hinges are rigid, which prevents the door from sagging the way it might if it were hanging on a concealed hinge with a long hinge arm. Full-wrap butt hinges provide the same appearance and no-sag benefits of butt hinges with the added benefit of being easier to install. These hinges often feature slotted and nonslotted screw holes for easy adjustment.

Wrap-around butt hinges also come in many different decorative styles. Some simply feature modestly ornamental hinge pins, while others boast amazingly filigreed tongues that are well-suited to period style or themed cabinetry with special finishes. As with pulls and handles, you should choose a butt hinge style that best suits the look and function of the cabinets you've selected. Butt hinges are very rarely used on frameless cabinets.

Because butt hinges are not self closing, you'll need to install either a mechanical latch, or a magnetic catch on the opening side of the face frame and door. Catches are far more popular than latches because they are quieter and require less precision to install.

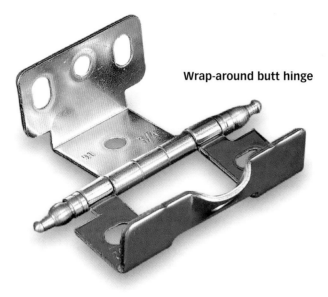

Wrap-around butt hinge

How to Install Wrap-around Butt Hinges

1

Install wrap-around hinges so that the top and bottom of the hinge barrel is 2 to 4" from the top or bottom (respectively) of the door. Mark the hinge locations on the back of the door.

Bore pilot holes through the centers of the slotted hinge holes only. Drive the hinge screws in the slotted holes to attach the hinge to the door.

Use a helper to center the door on the face-frame stile, holding the hinge plates against the stile. Bore pilot holes in the slotted hinge holes and then drive the hinge screws in the pilot holes. Once the door is fully mounted, centered in the face frame and operating properly, drive screws in the nonslotted holes to lock the door in place.

Attach a magnetic catch near the top of the door. Adjust the position of the catch so that the door is flush with the face frame when closed.

Door and Drawer Hardware

KNOBS & PULLS

Despite their small size, knobs and pulls play a major role in defining the style of the cabinets. Simply replacing the knobs is sometimes enough to refresh the appearance of dated or worn-out cabinets.

There is no rule dictating whether to use knobs or pulls on your doors. It's really up to your personal taste. You can use the same knobs or pulls on both drawers and doors or use a combination of knobs and pulls, such as pulls on the drawers and knobs on the doors. Pulls are easier to grab and a better choice if the homeowner has less hand strength.

It's important to install all the knobs or pulls in exactly the same place on every door. The best method is to use a hole-alignment jig to drill the pilot holes. You can make a simple jig using scrap wood or clear plastic, or you can purchase a manufactured jig.

How to Install Pulls

Use a jig to consistently mark positions for the pilot holes you'll need to drill in order to install the knobs or pulls. You can find these at hardware stores and home centers.

Position a backer board behind the door frame in the drilling area. A backer board prevents blowout in the wood on the backside of the hole. Drill guide holes for the knobs or pulls at the positions you've marked. Install the pull or knob with the mounting bolt that comes with the hardware.

CATCHES

Most butt hinges do not feature self-closing mechanisms, so they require a catch to keep the door from opening at unwanted times. In most cases, the catch should be installed at the top and near the outside end of the door.

Self-closing hinges do not require a catch, but you can add a high-end touch by installing a soft-close piston. This easy-to-install accessory stops a closing door about ½" before it hits the cabinet and then gently closes it against the cabinet, eliminating banging doors.

Catches & Soft Closers

Hinge-mounted soft closers fit on a specific matching brand and model of hinge.

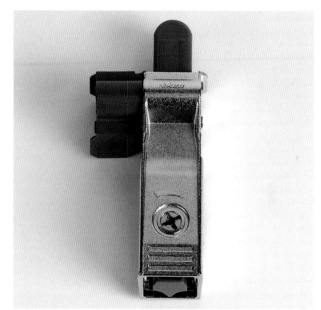

Cabinet mounted soft closers turn a door mounted on self-closing hinges into a soft closing door.

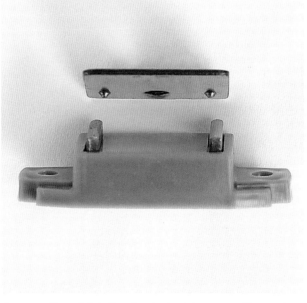

A magnetic catch is the standard catch to use with any door that is not mounted on a self-closing hinge.

A touch latch pops open the door with a gentle tap on the front of the door—no knob or pulls necessary.

Bathroom Window Seat

Two things that many bathrooms (and other rooms for that matter) lack are adequate storage and a comfortable place to sit. This built-in window-seat bench is especially designed to address both those inadequacies. The drawer is deep enough to hold three or four large towels or a family-sized collection of toiletries. The bench is just the right height for taking a seat while you get dressed, and with the addition of a seat cushion it will be comfortable enough for lounging. You can build the bench to fit a common cushion size or you can make your own cushion to fit the bench.

This bench design will look most natural and meet your particular needs best if you customize it to fit the space you have. This will mean taking some measurements and calculating the dimensions for your project based on your available space. Also, some parts are optional depending on where the bench is installed. For example, if the bench is installed with a vanity directly against one side but the other side is open and exposed, you will need to make a seat side edge piece and a side finished panel. But if the bench is captured between two taller objects, such as a vanity and a tub with a high sidewall, then you won't see the sides and do not need the side trim or finished panel.

Tools & Materials ▶

Table saw or circular saw
Router table or table saw
Cordless power drill
No. 8 pilot and countersink drill bit
Pneumatic brad nail gun and compressor (or hammer)
Wood glue
¼"-dia. straight router bit or ¼"-wide dado blade set
(1) ¼ × 2 × 4, birch veneer plywood (cabinet back)
(1) ¾ × 4 × 8, birch veneer plywood (bench cabinet sides, top and bottom)

(1) ½ × 4 × 4, Baltic birch plywood
(1) 1× 6 × 8, solid wood (face frames)
(1) 1 × 2 × 8, solid wood (seat edge)
(1 pr.) 18" drawer slides
1¼" wood screws
2" wood screws
1" panhead screws and washers
1" brad nails
1½" brad nails
Optional:
(1) ¼ × 2 × 4, veneer plywood (finish end; same species as solid wood)
Eye and ear protection
Work gloves

This built-in bench tucks in snugly next to a vanity cabinet and in front of a window. Fitted with a comfortable cushion, it provides convenient seating for getting dressed, and the ample storage is always a welcome addition to a bathroom.

Cutting List

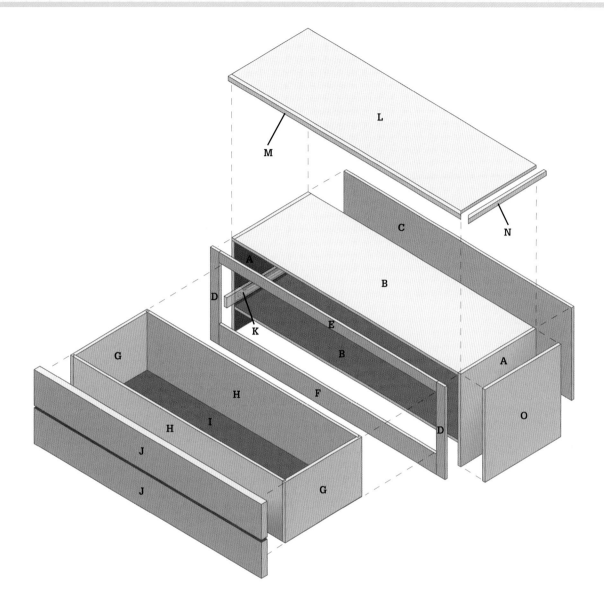

KEY	NO.	PART	DIMENSION
A	2	Cabinet sides	¾ × 16 × 18½"
B	2	Cabinet top/bottom	¾ × 18½ × (Y − 2)"
C	1	Back	¼ × 12¾ × (Y − 2)"
D	2	Stiles	¾ × 1¾ × 16"
E	1	Top rail	¾ × 1¾ × (Y − (3½))"
F	1	Bottom rail	¾ × 4 × (Y − (3½))"
G	2	Drawer box sides	½ × 9 × 18"
H	2	Drawer box front/back	½ × 9 × (Y − 5)"
I	1	Drawer box bottom	½ × 17½ × (Y − 5)"

KEY	NO.	PART	DIMENSION
J	2	Drawer fronts	¾ × 5½ × (Y − (2¾))"
K	2	Drawer slide cleats	¾ × 2 × 18¼"
L	1	Seat (without side trim)	¾ × 19½ × (Y + ¼)"
M	1	Seat front edge	¾ × 1 × (cut to fit)"
N	1	Seat side edge (Opt.)	¾ × 1 × 20"
O	1	Side finished panel (Opt.)	¼ × 16 × 18½"

* Y = width of opening for built-in (see step 1, next page)

How to Build a Bathroom Window Seat

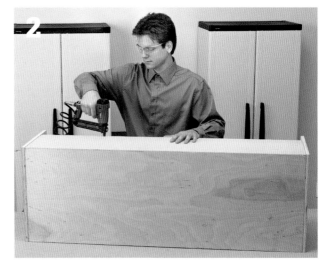

Measure the width of the space where you plan to install the cabinet. Measure in several places and record the smallest measurement. Plug this measurement in as Y in the cutting list equations to determine your part dimensions. To alter the cabinet width, you'll need to adjust the length (by a consistent amount) of the cabinet top, bottom and back panels, the top and bottom rails, the seat and the drawers. Identify obstacles, such as electrical outlets or HVAC registers, that will have to be removed or relocated for the bench to be installed.

Apply glue to the back edges of the top and bottom. Then place the back between the sides on the back edges of the top and bottom. Use a table saw and straightedge guide to cut the pieces to size. Place them on a flat work surface with the front edges down. Align the top face of the top with the top edges of the sides and position the top face of the bottom so it is 4" from the bottom edge of the sides. Attach the sides to the top and bottom with 2" flathead wood screws. Drill a pilot hole and countersink at each screw location. Adjust the cabinet so it is square and then attach the back with glue and 1" brads or 18-ga. pneumatic nails.

Cut the face-frame rails and stiles to size. Use a pocket-hole jig and drill bit to bore the pocket holes in the rails. Then assemble the face-frame with pocket screws. Attach the face frame to the cabinet with glue and 1½" brads. The outside edges of the face frame overhang the bench cabinet sides by ¼". The inside edges of the face frame overhang the inside faces of the cabinet sides by ¾".

Place the drawer side face down on the router table and use a miter gauge to guide the piece through the cut. Cut a ¼ × ¼" dado located ¼" from each end of the inside face.

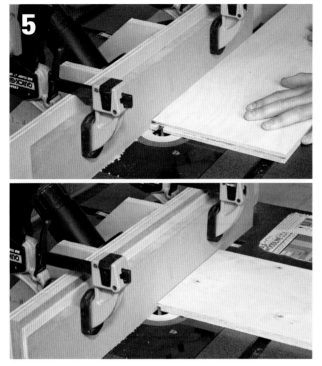

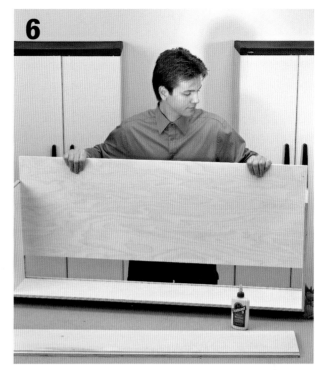

Cut the ½"-wide × ¼"-deep grooves that will contain the bottom in the front, back, and side pieces (top photo). Cut the groove in two passes. Test the fit of the drawer bottom in the groove. If the groove is too narrow, move the fence out slightly and make another pass to widen the groove. Then, cut the ¼ × ¼" rabbets in the ends of the front and back pieces. Place each piece face down and use a miter gauge to push it through the cut. Test-cut a rabbet in a scrap piece first, to check how well the rabbet fits in the drawer side-piece dado.

Dry-assemble the drawer, using clamps to hold the parts, to make sure all the parts fit together well. Assemble the drawer with glue, adjusting the parts and clamps as necessary to make them square (perpendicular and parallel) to each other.

Mount the drawer slides (see page 55). Bore ³⁄₁₆"-dia. pilot holes through the drawer box fronts. Then attach the drawer faces with No. 8 × 1" panhead screws and washers. Use 4 to 6 screws per drawer face, depending on how large the faces are.

Attach the top to the bench with 1¼" screws. When installing, use shims to fill any gaps between the side of the bench and the vanity or other flat surface and attach the cabinet to the vanity with 1½" screws. If you would like to integrate the look of the bench with the vanity, wrap the base with the same base molding that is used on the walls.

Recessed Cabinet

If you've got a recessed wall area that you're not sure how to use, a built-in cabinet might be a perfect fit. For example, the set-back space created on one or both sides of a bumped-out fireplace is a perfect spot to install a built-in cabinet.

Building a recessed cabinet is very similar to building a freestanding cabinet. The key difference is that a recessed cabinet must fit perfectly between the side walls. The easiest way to make a cabinet that will fit correctly is to make a basic interior cabinet case that's slightly smaller than the available space and then build a face frame and top cover that will cover the edges of the cabinet and fit snugly against the walls. The secret to achieving a perfect fit is to make the face frame and top slightly oversized and then scribe them to fit against the walls.

You can build a recessed cabinet with or without doors. In the version seen here, glass panel doors were built, but you can also use solid, natural wood veneer, or painted plywood panels to conceal the cabinet interior. It is important to purchase tempered glass when you are building glass panel doors. Tempered glass is treated with heat so that if it is broken, it will shatter into small pieces that are less likely to cause serious cuts. It's also stronger. You can't cut it yourself, so be sure to get the size correct when you order it cut-to-fit.

Building this cabinet requires intermediate woodworking skills and a few woodworking power tools, including a table saw, miter saw, and router table.

Tools & Materials ▶

Table saw
Miter saw
Power drill
Pocket hole jig kit
Finish or random orbit sander
Eye and ear protection
Work gloves

Doors:
Router table
Rail and stile router bit set
⅜"-rad. rabbet bottom-bearing router bit

**Cabinet materials (to make one roughly
    4-ft.-wide × 4-ft.-tall × 12"-deep cabinet):**
(2) 2 × 4 × 8-ft. pine
(1) ¼ × 4 × 8 plain-sawn cherry veneer plywood

(1) ¾ × 4 × 8 plain-sawn cherry veneer plywood
(2) ¾ × 1½" × 8-ft. cherry
(2) ¾ × 2½" × 8-ft. cherry
(1) ¾ × 5 × 48" cherry
2" flat-head wood screws
2½" flat-head wood screws
1¼" fine thread washer-head (pocket) screws
18-ga. × 2" brad nails
(24) ¼"-dia. shelf pins

Doors (to make four roughly 11 × 46" doors):
(5) ¾ × 2" × 8-ft. solid cherry
(1) ¾ × 4 × 30 solid cherry
(4 pr.) nonmortise full-wrap hinges
(4) ⅛"-thick tempered glass panels
(4) magnetic door catches
18-ga. × ¾" brad nails

Cutting List

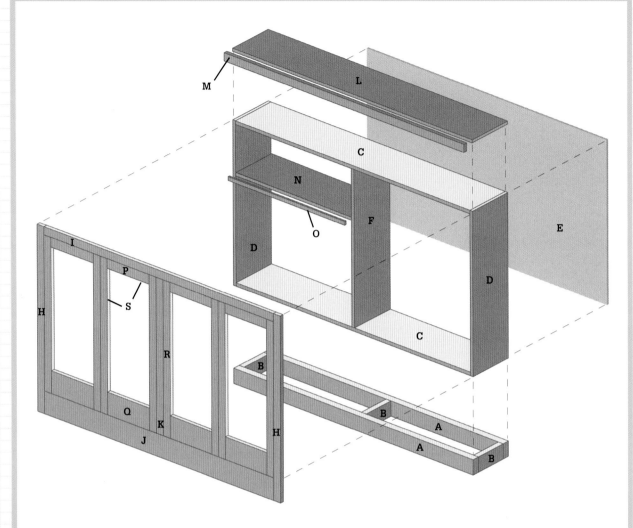

KEY	NO.	DESCRIPTION	DIMENSION
Cabinet			
A	2	Base rails	1½ × 3½ × 46"
B	3	Base cross pieces	1½ × 3½ × 8¼"
C	2	Cabinet top and bottom	¾ × 11 × 43½"
D	2	Cabinet sides	¾ × 11 × 48"
E	1	Cabinet back	¼ × 45 × 48"
F	1	Cabinet divider	¾ × 11 × 46½"
G	2	Back cleats	¾ × 2½ × 43½"
H	2	Face-frame stiles	¾ × 2½ × 51½"
I	1	Face-frame top rail	¾ × 2½ × 43"
J	1	Face-frame bottom rail	¾ × 4¼ × 43"

KEY	NO.	DESCRIPTION	DIMENSION
K	1	Face-frame center stile	¾ × 2¾ × 45¼"
L	1	Top	¾ × 11¾ × 48"
M	1	Top front edge	¾ × 1¼ × 48"
N	6	Shelf	¾ × 11 × 43¼"
O	6	Shelf edge	¾ × 1 × 43¼"
P	4	Top rail	¾ × 1⅝ × 6⅝"
Q	4	Bottom rail	¾ × 3⅝ × 6⅝"
R	8	Stiles	¾ × 2 × 44½"
S	16	Glass tack strips	¼ × ¼" × glass perimeter

How to Build a Recessed Cabinet

Measure the width of the space where the cabinet will be installed. Measure at several heights above the floor and at the front and back of the space. Record and use the smallest measurement. **Note:** You'll need to limit the shelf lengths to no more than 30" long—any span larger than that and they are likely to sag and break. Shorten shelf lengths in a wide cabinet by dividing the cabinet into multiple sections with vertical divider panels. Also use vertical dividers if you plan to store heavy objects on the shelves.

Cut the base frame parts to length and assemble the base with 2½" wood screws. Center the base between the side walls and against the back wall. Level the base with shims and then attach it to the back wall. Drive 3" drywall screws through the back base rail and into the wall studs. Trim off any exposed shims flush with the front edge of the base.

Cut the cabinet sides, dividers, top, and bottom. Bore the shelf-pin holes and cut the back cleats to length. Sand each part and attach the sides to the top and bottom with 2" wood screws. Bore pilot holes before driving screws into plywood edges. Attach the back cleats to the sides and top with 2" wood screws. Attach the divider panels to the top and bottom with 2" screws. Use a square to make sure the divider is perpendicular to the top and bottom. Bore a pilot hole and countersink hole for each screw. Drive the screws through the top and bottom.

Attach the back panel with glue and 1" brads. Keep the cabinet sides, top, and bottom perpendicular as you attach the back panel. Place the cabinet frame on the base. Center the cabinet on the base and align the front edge of the cabinet with the front edge of the base.

(continued)

Attach the cabinet to the wall. Bore a pilot and countersink hole through the back cleat and side panels at each stud location. Place scrap blocks or shims behind each screw hole to fill the gap between the wall and cabinet. Secure the cabinet with 3" drywall screws.

The face frame and top are made to fit exactly between the walls and will cover the gaps that were left between the cabinet and walls. Cut the face-frame stiles and rails to size. Temporarily attach the rails to the cabinet with tape. Then, scribe the stiles to follow the profile of the wall. Hold the stile perpendicular to the rails and against the side wall. Set a compass opening to match the distance that the stile overlaps the ends of the rails.

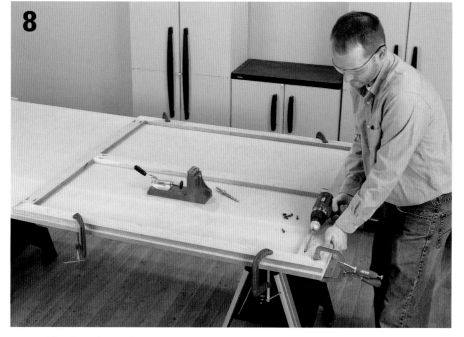

Hold the metal point of the compass against the wall and pull the compass down along the wall to trace the profile of the wall onto the face of the stile. The stile must remain perpendicular to the rails as you draw the scribe line. Follow the same process to scribe the other stile. Trim the stiles along the scribe lines.

Assemble the cabinet face frame with pocket screws. Clamp the parts to a large work surface to keep them perpendicular as they are connected. Sand the face frame smooth. Attach the face frame to the cabinet frame with glue and a few 18 ga. × 1¼" brads.

Tape together pieces of paper or cardboard to make a template for the top. Leave a ⅛" space between the template and the walls. Then, trace the template on the top panel stock and cut out the top. Cut the top front edge piece the same length as the front edge of the top panel. Attach the top front edge to the top with glue.

Clamp the front edge until the glue has cured. Remove the clamps, sand the top assembly, and attach the top to the cabinet with 1¼" screws. Drive the screws through the underside of the cabinet top panel and into the finished top. Use one screw in each corner and two screws evenly spaced near the front and back of the cabinet.

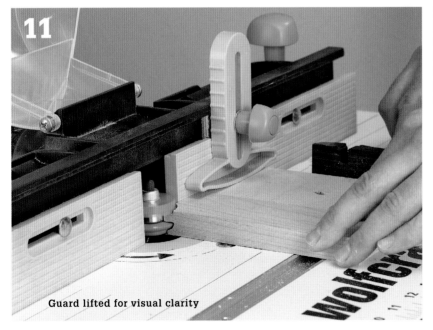

Guard lifted for visual clarity

This router bit set cuts a ⅜"–long stub tenon. The extra ¾" necessary for the two stub tenons must be added to the length of the rails. Rout the stub tenons on the ends of the rails. Set the router bit height so the top cutter will mill a ⅛"-deep rabbet above the stub tenon.

(continued)

12

Rout the groove profile in the inside edges of the rails and stiles. Set the router bit height to align the groove with the stub tenon (inset). Make test cuts in a scrap piece to adjust the bit height for a perfect fit before cutting the actual parts.

13

Assemble the door frame with glue. Measure diagonally across the corners to check the frame for square.

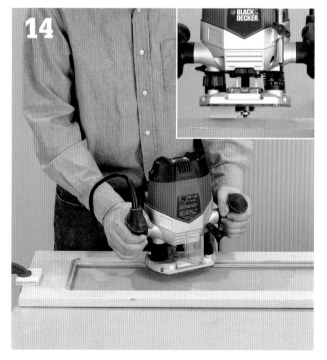

14

Use a chisel to clean up the corners of the rabbet that the router bit does not reach. Use a bottom-bearing rabbet bit to remove the back lip of the groove. Set the bit depth so that the bearing rides on the front edge or "stick" profile of the door (inset).

15

16

Fasten the hinge to the door using the slotted screw holes first. These holes allow you to adjust the door position slightly. Drive screws in the fixed screw holes after the door is positioned correctly in the cabinet. Drill pilot holes for each screw to prevent stripping the screw head, breaking the screws or splitting the door stile.

Install the glass in the doors after the finish is dry. Place a sheet of glass in each door. Cut the tack strips to fit along each side of the glass. Bore ¹⁄₃₂"-dia. pilot holes through the tack strips, spacing them 6" apart. Place the strips over the glass and drive an 18 ga. × ¾" brad nail into each pilot hole. Use a brad push tool to drive the brads or gently tap the brads with a small hammer. Cover the glass with a piece of cardboard to protect it.

Door Dimensions ▶

To prevent sagging, the maximum width of each door should be less than 24". If the cabinet opening is greater than 24" wide, use two doors. The bottom rail is wider than the top rail for two reasons. First, a wider bottom rail gives the door good scale by adding a little more visual weight to the bottom of the door. Second, the wider dimension adds more gluing surface, creating a stronger frame to support the glass panel.

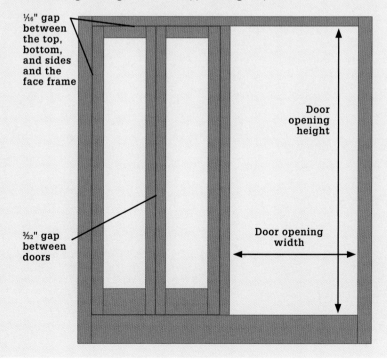

¹⁄₁₆" gap between the top, bottom, and sides and the face frame

³⁄₃₂" gap between doors

Door opening height

Door opening width

Door overall dimensions:

Door width = face-frame opening width – side gaps (¹⁄₁₆ sides and ³⁄₃₂ between doors)

Door height = face-frame opening height – top and bottom gaps (⅛ total)

Door part dimensions:

Door stile length = height of door

Door rail length = width of door – 2 (stile width) + 2 (tenon length)

Media Bar

Your snacks and beverages will always be close at hand during the big game when your flat-panel TV is mounted in this media cabinet. It combines the functionality of an entertainment center and the convenience of a mini kitchen. The base and upper cabinets provide storage for your home theater components, movies, games, and snacks. There's also a space between the base cabinets for a small refrigerator or beverage cooler. The counter serves as a perfect serving station or a place to keep a couple additional small appliances, such as a microwave or blender. And, the integrated matching wood wall conceals a structural frame that is easy to mount your TV to and provides a path for cables from the TV to your electronic components in the base cabinet.

This unit may look like a custom-built piece of furniture, but it's actually made from a combination of stock kitchen cabinets and matching cover panels. Building it only requires a few portable power tools and basic building skills.

Tools & Materials ▸

Table saw or circular saw and straightedge
Jigsaw
Power drill
Level
2"-dia. hole saw bit
Drill bits (⅛, ¼")
Caulk gun
(5) 2 × 4 × 8-ft.
(2) 1 × 4 × 8-ft.
Screws (1¼, 2, 2½")
Panel adhesive
(1) ½" × 4 × 8 finish-grade plywood
(3) 24" base cabinets
(2) 24" wall cabinets
(1) 25½" × 8 ft. countertop
Eye and ear protection
Work gloves

Cutting List

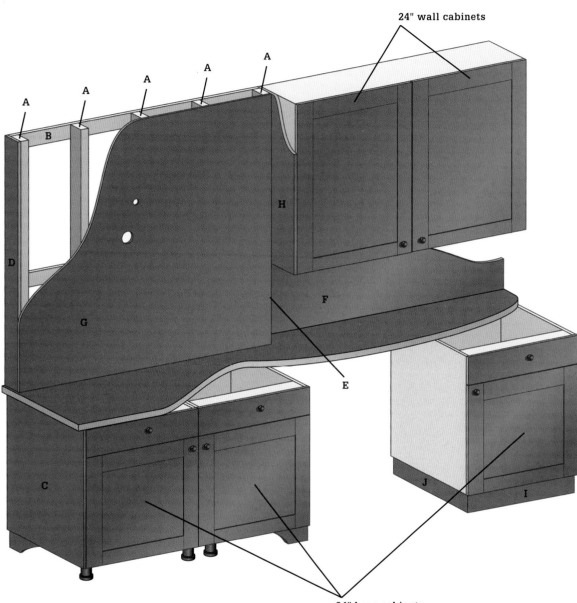

24" wall cabinets

A A A A A

B

D

G

H

F

E

C

J

I

24" base cabinets

KEY	NO.	DESCRIPTION	DIMENSION	KEY	NO.	DESCRIPTION	DIMENSION
A	5	Wall frame studs	1½ × 3½ × 60"	**F**	1	Back splash panels	½ × 20 × 48"
B	3	Wall frame cleats	¾ × 3½ × 47"	**G**	1	Wall frame front cover panels	½ × 48 × 60"
C	1	Base cabinet cover panel	½ × 24 × 30"	**H**	1	Wall cabinet side cover panel	½ × 8⅝ × 40"
D	1	Left frame side cover panel	½ × 4¼ × 60"	**I**	1	Front-toe kick	½ × 4½* × 24"
E	1	Right frame side cover panel	½ × 4¼ × 20"	**J**	1 or 2	Side-toe kick	½ × 4½* × 24"

How to Build a Media Bar

Install any necessary electrical outlets and cables or wire before you install the cabinets. Locate and mark the wall stud locations. Assemble wall and base cabinet frames if they are not pre-assembled. Wait to install doors and drawers until the cover panels are attached. Install the wall cabinets. In this case a metal bracket is attached to the wall and the cabinets are fastened to the metal bracket. Attach the cabinets to each other with fasteners provided by the cabinet manufacturer or by driving short screws through the cabinet sides.

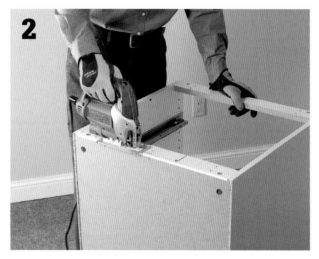

Cut access holes in the base cabinet. Trace outlines for the access holes in the back panel and top spreader on the cabinet that will be installed in front of the wall outlet. Drill ⅜"-dia. saw blade starter holes at each corner of the outline. Use a jigsaw to cut the sides of the hole.

Position base cabinets against the wall and level them. Screw them together and then to the wall. Cut the countertop access hole. Attach masking tape to the countertop to help prevent chipping the surface when it is cut. Mark the access notch outline on the countertop. Cut the notch with a jigsaw.

Attach the countertop to the cabinets. Drive 1⅝" screws through the cabinet top and into the countertop. Be careful not to overdrive the screws and break through the top surface of the countertop. **Note:** Natural stone countertop materials require a diamond abrasive blade and should be cut by a stone countertop fabricator.

Cut the 2 × 4 wall frame posts and 1 × 4 cleats to length and assemble them with 2" wood screws. Then place the wall frame on the countertop and against the wall cabinet. Attach the frame to the wall. Drive 2½" drywall screws through the wall frame cleats and into the room wall studs. Drive three screws into each stud.

(continued)

6

Cut the backsplash panels to size using a plywood cutting blade with a high tooth count to prevent the finished surface from chipping. Cut any outlet openings and attach the backsplash panels with panel adhesive. Attach the wall frame side cover panels to the wall frame with panel adhesive and 1⅝" screws. Clamp the panels in position while you drive the screws through the inside face of the wall frame posts. Drill a ⅛"-dia. pilot hole and countersink for each screw.

7

Cut the wall frame front panels to size. The cover panel stock features one finished edge. Install the panels with the finished edges on the outside and the unfinished edges butted together at the middle seam. Attach the panels to the frame with panel adhesive. Measure the distance from the face of the front panel to the front edge of the wall cabinet. Add the thickness of the door to determine the width of the wall cabinet side cover panel.

Cut the wall cabinet side cover panel to size. Attach the wall and base cabinet side panels. Clamp the panel to the cabinet side and drive 1" screws through the inside face of the cabinet side. Then install the toe-kick panels, doors, and drawers.

Use a 2" hole saw to bore an access hole through the wall frame front panel. This hole should be located directly above the notch in the countertop and close to the TV mounting bracket so that the TV will conceal it. Follow the manufacturer instructions to install the TV mounting bracket. Fish the component cables and speaker cable through the access holes and behind the front panels. Follow the manufacturer instructions to secure the TV to the mounting bracket and mount the speaker.

Full-Height Medicine Cabinet

A classic medicine chest is a great storage solution for several reasons. First, it keeps your personal care products right where you need them—near the sink. Second, its multiple shallow shelves store small items in plain view, so there's no digging around for everyday necessities. Built-in medicine cabinets are recessed into the wall, minimizing the impact on the room's precious floor space. And finally, most medicine chests serve a dual purpose in the bathroom by incorporating mirrored doors.

Indeed, the basic medicine chest design leaves little room for improvement. That's why the bathroom cabinet in this project takes the same great features and simply makes more of them. This built-in cabinet has a 3½"-deep storage space yet projects only ¾" from the wall (not counting the overhead crown molding). Inside, it's loaded with adjustable shelves, so it can hold not only prescription bottles and toiletries, but also taller items like shampoo bottles and cleaning supplies. And the cabinet's door is tall enough to accommodate a full-length mirror—a great convenience feature for any bathroom.

The box of this medicine cabinet is sized to fit into a standard 14½"-wide space between wall studs. With the drywall cut away, the box slips into place and mounts directly to the studs. Then you trim out the cabinet to fit the style of your bathroom. The traditional molding treatment shown here is only one way to do it; you can add any type of molding and extras you like using the same techniques. Another option is to build a similar cabinet that mounts to the surface of the wall, as shown in the variation on page 139. With this design, you're not limited by the width and depth of a stud cavity, but the cabinet will occupy a greater amount of floor space.

Tools & Materials ▸

Work gloves	AC plywood
Eye and ear	(¼", ¾")
protection	Poplar (1 × 4, 1 × 6)
Tape measure	Shims
Circular saw	Pegboard
Miter saw	Shelf pins
Power drill	Door catch
Clamps	Finish nails
Chisel	(1½, 2¼")
Mallet	Construction
Drywall saw	adhesive
Putty knife	Mirror
Level	(approx. 10 × 48")
Drill guide	Wood putty
Paint brush	Finishing materials
Caulk gun	Crown molding

Using less than two feet of wall space, this built-in cabinet offers more than enough room for a household's medicines, toiletries, and backup bathroom supplies.

Tools & Materials

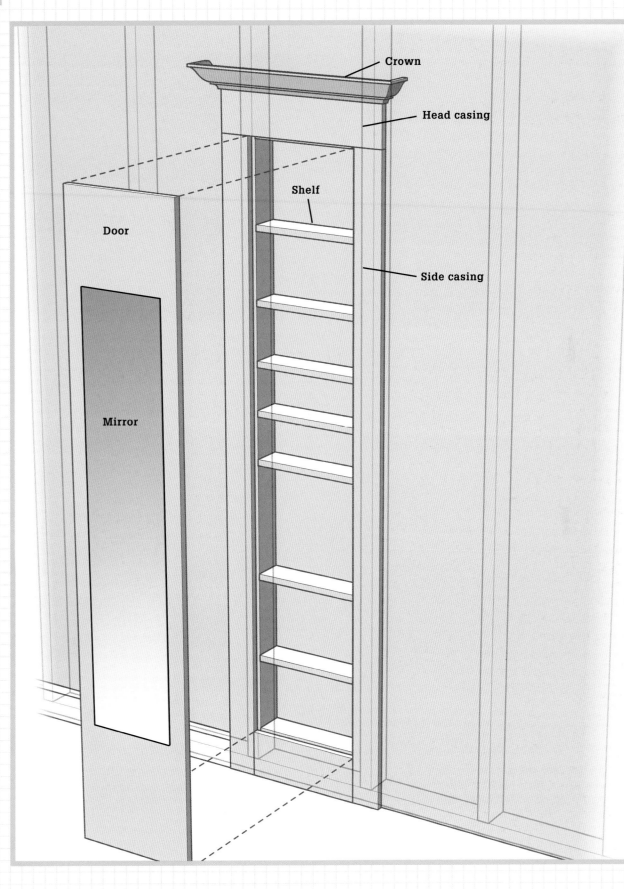

Crown

Head casing

Shelf

Side casing

Door

Mirror

How to Build & Install a Full-Height Medicine Cabinet

1

Determine the overall height of the finished cabinet (with trim), then subtract the height of the trim assembly above the door. Add ¼" to find the height of the cabinet box. Measure up from the floor and draw a level line at the installed box height between two wall studs where the cabinet will go.

2

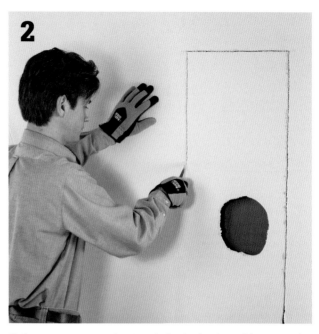

Cut one or more exploratory holes in the drywall between the host studs, then examine the stud cavity to make sure that no electrical cables, plumbing pipes, or other elements intersect the cavity. Cut out the drywall between the studs, up to the level line.

3

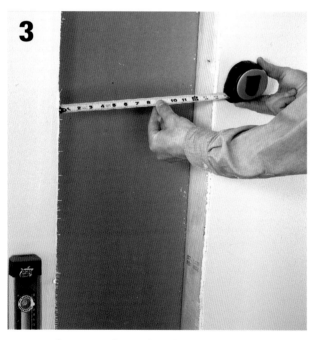

Measure between the studs to determine the overall width of the cabinet box. **Tip:** If the studs aren't plumb, leave some extra room for adjusting the cabinet when you install it (see step 8, on page 137).

4

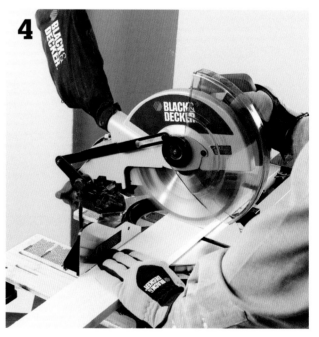

Cut the two side pieces for the cabinet box to length, 1½" shorter than the floor-to-top dimension from step 1. Cut the top piece, middle shelf, and bottom shelf 1½" shorter than the overall cabinet width. Cut the adjustable shelves ³⁄₁₆" shorter than the fixed shelves. Cut the back panel equal to the overall width of the cabinet and the same length as the sides.

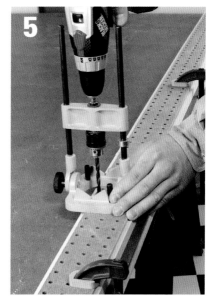

Drill holes into the box sides for the adjustable shelf pins, using pegboard with ¼" holes as a drilling guide. Align the pegboard so that the hole pairs are evenly spaced across each side piece, and drill the holes to the depth of the pin plus the hardboard, using a stop collar on the bit. Make sure the hole pairs are matched on both pieces so the shelves will hang level.

Assemble the cabinet box by fastening the sides over the ends of the top and bottom and middle shelves using glue and 2" screws. Position the bottom shelf so its top face is 4½" from the ends of the sides. Position the top piece flush with the top ends of the sides, and position the middle shelf roughly halfway in between.

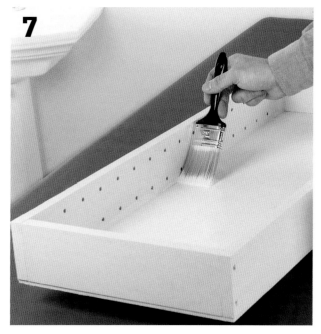

Fasten the back panel to the assembly with 1" screws. Align the box sides and top with the panel edges as you work to ensure the assembly is square. Prime all sides of the box, including the back, and then add two top coats of paint to the box interior and front edges of the side pieces.

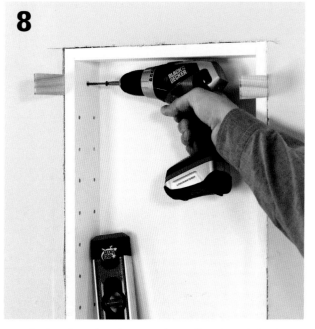

Set the box into place between the wall studs and check it for plumb. Use shims to fill any gaps along the studs and to adjust for plumb. Fasten the box sides to the studs with 2" screws so the front edges of the sides are flush with the surface of the drywall.

(continued)

9

Cut, prime, and install the 1 × 4 side trim and 1 × 6 base trim with 2¼" finish nails, overlapping the sides of the box by ¼". Add the bead and head trim over the ends of the side trim. Install the crown molding over the head trim with 1½" finish nails, mitering the corners and adding return pieces back to the wall. Measure the opening created by the trim pieces and cut the door panel ⅛" narrower and shorter than the opening.

10

Fill any voids in the panel edges with wood putty, sand the panel smooth, and prime and paint the panel. Paint the cabinet trim, and fill and paint over the screw heads inside the cabinet box.

11

Mount the door to the side trim with three small butt hinges or a single piano hinge. Mortise-in butt hinges for a flush fit. Install a drawer pull or knob, then add a magnetic door catch onto the door and cabinet box side.

12

Have the mirror cut to the desired size by a glass dealer. Secure the mirror to the front of the door panel with a recommended adhesive (you can remove the door if you used butt hinges). If desired, add trim around the edges of the mirror. Install the adjustable shelves.

Variation: Surface-Mount Cabinet ▸

This surface-mount cabinet is a freestanding unit that you secure to the wall for stability. You can use this design if a recessed cabinet is impractical or undesirable for your situation. The basic construction steps are similar to those of the recessed unit:

1. Assemble the cabinet box with a fixed top, middle shelf, bottom shelf, and back panel. If you want a deeper cabinet and it won't impede critical floorspace in the room, you can substitute 1 × 6 lumber for the box sides, top, and shelves.

2. Add 1 × 2 side trim pieces to the front of the box, then add a 1 × 4 head trim piece and a 1 × 6 base trim piece between the side trim. Cut the door to fit between the side, head, and base trim pieces.

3. Add the crown molding, then prime and paint all parts. Hang the door with hinges secured to the side trim.

4. Secure the cabinet to a wall stud with screws driven through the back panel. Wrap the base of the cabinet with baseboard trim for a built-in look. Add quarter-round molding along the cabinet sides to hide the edges of the back panel and any gapping caused by wall contours.

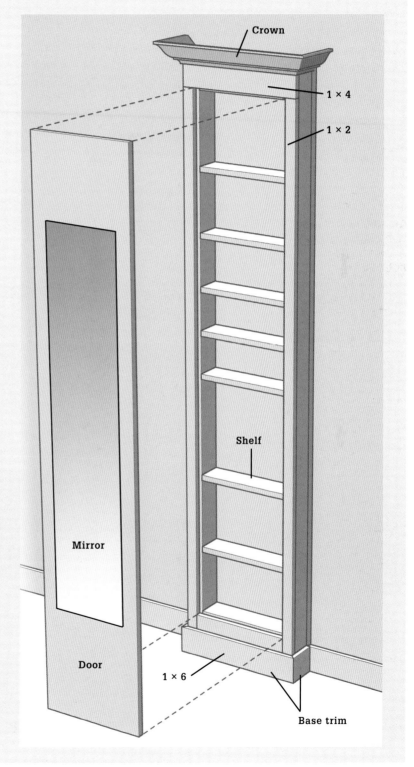

Custom Laundry Center

Many laundry rooms—or set-aside laundry areas in larger rooms—lack two vitally important features: organization and lighting. This laundry center answers both needs in style. This is a self-contained built-in that functions like a room within a room, adding both storage space and task lighting for what can otherwise be a disagreeable task. It is built from a base cabinet and butcher block countertop on one side of a 24"-wide, 7 ft.-tall stub wall, and a bank of wall cabinets on the other side of the wall. The cabinets are designed to fit above a washer and dryer combo, although you may need to adjust the measurements to accommodate your particular washer and dryer.

The structure includes a ceiling with light fixtures mounted over both sides, and a switch wired into the stub wall to control the lights. The walls are built from inexpensive wall sheathing and, along with the ceiling, are clad with easy-to-wash tileboard that adds brightness while contrasting with the maple wood of the cabinets. The edges of the center are trimmed with clear maple.

Tools & Materials ▶

Tape measure
Level
Pencil
Square
Power drill and bits
Powder-actuated
  nailer
Hammer or
  pneumatic nailer
Jigsaw
Circular saw
Miter saw
Eye and ear
  protection
Work gloves

This sharp cabinet configuration not only helps you get your laundry room in order, but it also adds a good deal of style and practical lighting.

Cutting List

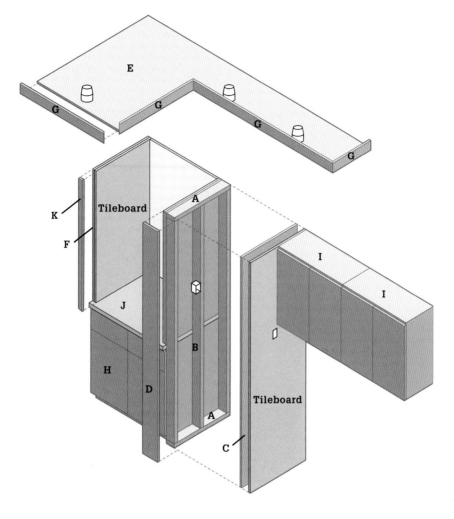

(1) 4 × 8 × ½ plywood or OSB (wall sheathing)
(1) 4 × 8 × ¾ plywood or OSB (ceiling)
(3) 4 × 8 sheets tileboard with an 8-ft. inside corner strip and panel adhesive
(3) Recessed canister light with trim kit
(1) Clothes rod (24") with mounting hardware
1 × 2, 1 × 4 and 1 × 6 maple for trim
32"-wide base cabinet
Butcher block countertop for base cabinet
(2) 30" 2-door uppers
Electrical box, switch, 14/2 romex, switch plate
End panel for upper cabinets (if unfinished)
Panel adhesive
Drywall or deck screws
Nails
(4) 1½ × 3½ × 96 pine

PART	NO.	DESC.	SIZE	MATERIAL
A	2	Cap/sill plate	1½ × 3½ × 23¾"	2 × 4
B	3	Stud	1½ × 3½ × 79"	2 × 4
C	1	Full wall	½ × 23¾ × 81¾"	Sheathing
D	1	Wall cap	¾ × 5½ × 79"	Maple 1 × 6
E	1	Ceiling	¾ × 24 × 100"*	Sheathing
F	2	Half wall	½ × 23¾ × 43"	Sheathing
G	4	Top trim	¾ × 5½ × cut to fit	Maple 1 × 6
H	1	Base cabinet	34½" h × 36" w	Stock cabinet
I	2	Wall cabinets	12 × 30 × 30"	Stock cabinets
J	1	Countertop	1½ × 25 × 36	Countertop
K	1	Trim	¾ × 1½ × 43"	1 × 2

*Can be pieced together from two boards joined above A

How to Build a Laundry Center

1

Attach the base plate for the stub wall perpendicular to the wall, allowing space between the stub wall and the corner for your base cabinet. Use pressure-treated wood if your laundry is in the basement and use pressure-treated lumber for the base plate and attach it by driving concrete nails with a powder-actuated nailer for a concrete floor.

2

After toenailing the studs to the base plate (and facenailing the stud next to the wall if possible), attach the cap plate, making sure the studs are vertical.

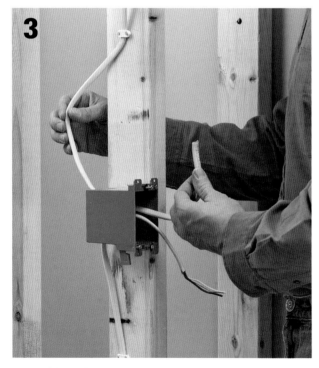

3

Run cable and install boxes for the light fixtures. Hire an electrician to do this if you are not experienced with home wiring. **Note:** You may need to apply for a permit and have your wiring inspected.

4

Install the base cabinet between the stub wall and the corner, making sure it is level and securely attached to at least one wall.

Attach the countertop material (butcher block was used here). The countertop should be flush against both walls and it should overhang the base cabinet slightly.

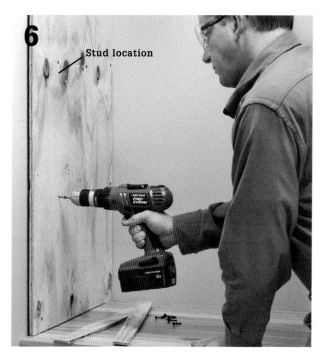

Stud location

Cut a piece of wall sheathing that's the same width as the stub wall and reaches the same height when placed on the countertop surface. Attach the sheathing to the side of the countertop area. Insert a couple of furring strips between the sheathing and the wall to create airspace.

Clad the stub wall on both sides with wall sheathing, making sure to cut out accurately for the switch box. The sheathing on the countertop side should rest on the countertop. Slip shims underneath the wall sheathing on the washer and dryer side so it does not contact the floor.

Cut pieces of tileboard to cover the wall surfaces and attach them with panel adhesive. Attach inside corner strips cut to fit at the inside corners of the countertop area. Rub the tileboard aggressively with rags to help seat it.

(continued)

Mount the wall cabinets so they are level and their tops are flush with the top of the stub wall and they butt up against the stub wall. Drive screws through the mounting strips and into the wall at stud locations or into ledgers.

It's easiest to cut the ceiling board, attach tileboard, and mount light fixtures before you attach the ceiling assembly to the stub wall and cabinets. Cut the ceiling board to size and shape from a piece of sheathing.

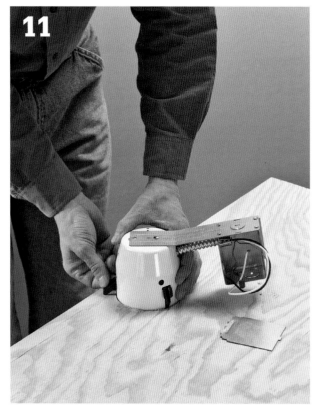

Mount the hardware and box for the light fixture to the ceiling panel before you install the ceiling.

Set the ceiling panel over the laundry center and attach it with nails or screws driven into the top plate of the stub wall and the cabinet sides.

13

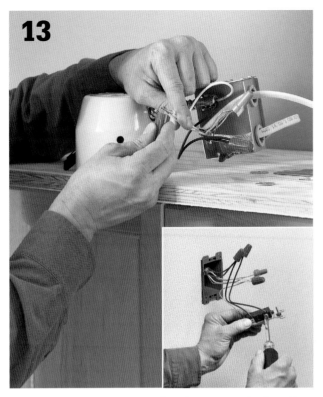

Be sure the power is turned off to the room. Make the wiring connections at the light fixtures and at the switch (inset). Consult an electrician as necessary.

14

Trim out the top of the structure with 1 × 4 hardwood to conceal the gap beneath the ceiling panel. Miter the outside and inside corners as you install the trim. If you prefer, you can use crown molding here.

15

Attach the vertical trim boards, butting them up against the top trim and keeping the bottom slightly above the floor. Apply a finish and top coat to the trim boards as desired.

16

Install your washer and dryer (or have your appliance dealer install them for you). Make sure to follow local codes for water and drain supply and for venting your dryer.

Compact Laundry Center

Although there may be no scientific evidence to prove it, we all know that there's a direct correlation between the quality of a laundry room space and how much we dread doing the laundry. Cramped, cluttered, or poorly arranged rooms slow the work and add a general sense of unpleasantness. And things get complicated when you can't complete the laundry tasks in the laundry room—you have to hang up your sweaters to dry over the bathtub and do all the folding on the kitchen table.

If this sounds all too familiar, you'll be glad to know that it doesn't take much to turn an ordinary laundry area into an efficient work center. Nor does it take a lot of space. The project shown here requires only about nine feet of wall area, including where the washer and dryer go. And with a few extra feet available on a nearby wall, you can add a hideaway ironing board that folds up into a recessed cabinet when not in use.

Tools & Materials ▸

Work gloves	Melamine-laminate	Polyurethane glue	2¼" finish nails
Eye and ear	wall cabinets	Coarse-thread drywall	Post-formed laminate
protection	(30" × 24" and	screws (1¼", 2")	countertop straight
4-ft. level	36" × 30")	Melamine-laminate	section, (48" long)
Power drill and bits	3½" heavy-duty	edge tape and	Countertop end cap kit
Circular saw and	wood screws	stickers	¾" particleboard
straightedge guide	¾" melamine-	Hanger rod with	Wood glue
Drywall saw	covered	mounting brackets	Ironing board cabinet
Plumb bob	particleboard	Lumber (1 × 2, 2 × 2)	for recessed wall
Stud finder	(laminated on	Deck screws	mounting
Household iron	both sides)	(3½", 2½")	Drop hook (optional)

What every laundry room needs: dedicated areas for ironing, hanging, folding, and stacking clothes, plus convenient spaces for holding point-of-use supplies and for stored items that you want to keep clean.

How to Create a Laundry Center

Mark the cabinet locations onto the wall, including level lines to represent the cabinets' top edges. Standard cabinet height is 84" above the floor, but make sure the washer door won't block the hanging shelf. Locate and mark all of the wall studs behind the cabinet locations.

Assemble the cabinets, if necessary. Position each cabinet with its top edge flush to the level line, drill pilot holes, and fasten through the back panel and into the wall studs with at least four 3½" heavy-duty wood screws (or install according to the manufacturer's directions).

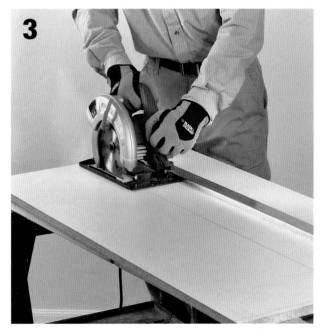

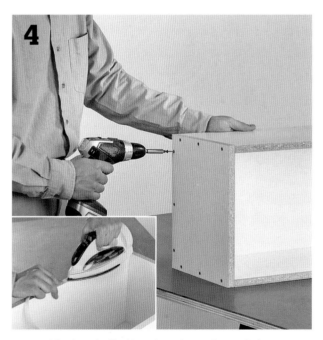

Cut pieces of ¾" melamine-covered particleboard for the hanging shelf. Cut the top and bottom pieces equal to the cabinet depth × the cabinet width minus 1½". Cut the side pieces equal to the cabinet depth × the overall shelf height (as desired). Cut the back panel equal to the cabinet depth × the shelf height minus 1½" in both directions.

Assemble the shelf with polyurethane glue and 2" coarse-thread drywall screws or particleboard screws. Cover any exposed front edges and screw heads with melamine-laminate edge tape and cosmetic stickers (inset). When the glue has cured, mount the shelf to the bottom cabinet panel with 1¼" coarse-thread drywall screws driven through pilot holes.

(continued)

5

Mount the hanger rod to the sides of the cabinets using the provided screws. Locate the rod as close as possible to the front edge of the cabinets (without hindering door operation) and as high as you can comfortably reach.

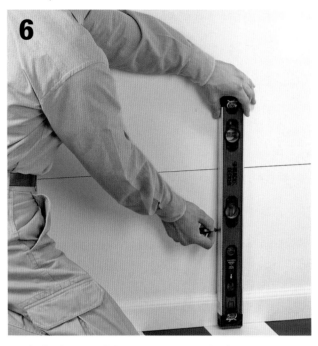

6

Mark the layout of the countertop and shelf unit onto the wall. Draw level lines at 34½" and at the desired height for the shelf top minus ¾". Draw plumb lines for the end panel at 46½ and 47¼" from the side wall and for the shelf support at 22⅞ and 23⅝" from the side wall. Also mark all wall studs in the area.

7

Following the layout lines, cut and install 2 × 2 wall cleats for the countertop along the back and side walls. Fasten the cleats to the wall studs with 3½" deck screws. Cut and install 1 × 2 cleats for the shelf, shelf support, and end panel using 2½" deck screws or drywall screws.

8

Build the end panel and shelf to size at 34½" long × the countertop depth minus ¾". Cut the shelf at 46½" long × the same width as the end panel. Add a 2 × 2 cleat flush with the top edge of the end panel. Fasten the shelf and end panel to the wall cleats with polyurethane glue and 2¼" finish nails. Fasten through the end panel and into the shelf edge with 2" screws.

Cut the shelf support to fit underneath the shelf. Notch the back edge to fit around the 1 × 2 wall cleat, then install the support to the cleat and shelf with glue and 2¼" finish nails.

Prepare the countertop by cutting a stiffener panel from ¾" particleboard to fit inside the edges on the underside of the countertop. Fasten the panel with wood glue and 1¼" screws. If desired, install an end cap kit onto the end opposite the side wall following the manufacturer's directions. Set the countertop in place and secure it to the 2 × 2 cleats with 2" screws.

Begin the ironing board cabinet installation by locating two adjacent wall studs and drawing level lines to mark the top and bottom of the wall opening. Make sure there's no wiring or plumbing inside the wall cavity, then cut the drywall along the stud edges and the level lines using a drywall saw.

Fit the cabinet into the wall opening and secure it to the wall studs using the recommended screws. **Tip:** Add a drop hook on the inside of the cabinet door for hanging up ironed clothes (inset). The hook drops down against the door when not in use.

Custom Double Vanity Cabinet

You can purchase vanity tops with a matching stock vanity cabinet, or you can put your own design stamp on the bathroom by building a custom vanity cabinet. Crafting a your own vanity cabinet is a great way to seamlessly integrate the unit into the overall bathroom design, especially when you haven't been able to find the cabinet of your dreams at retail.

The custom double cabinet in this project was designed to support a stock double-bowl vanity. The cabinet is built with ½", 9-ply Baltic birch plywood and solid birch framing. This particular plywood is a favorite of cabinetmakers because of its beautiful grain structure and appealing edge appearance. The look of the finished cabinet is contemporary and clean, making it suitable to a wide range of bathroom decors. The unit is wall mounted, but two legs at the front of the cabinet provide stability and create the appearance of a standalone piece of furniture.

All panels are cut with the grain running horizontally. The doors offer easy access to the abundant storage space inside the cabinet, and the bottom drawer is operable while the top is a false front. The project requires moderate woodworking skills and precise measurements. But with a little effort, you'll wind up with gorgeous vanity cabinetry that is uniquely your own.

This custom-made cabinet is built using Baltic birch plywood for a clean, contemporary feel. Because it is wall-hung, it feels open and light, but the front legs guarantee that it is stable.

Tools & Materials & Cutting List ▸

Circular saw
Router
Drill
Door pulls
Pocket jig
2" flathead wood
   screws
3/8" × 3½" lag screws
   with washers
½" Baltic birch
   plywood
½" plywood
Self-closing cup
   hinges
2 self-leveling 10"
   furniture legs
Bottom-mount drawer
   slide
2 × 4
1½" finish nails
No. 8 × ¾" panhead
   screws

KEY	NO.	PART	SIZE	MATERIAL
A	2	Door	½ × 23¾ × 19"	Baltic birch
B	2	Drawer fronts	½ × 12 × 9¾"	Baltic birch
C	2	End Panels	½ × 12 × 20"	Baltic birch
D	1	Bottom panel	½ × 19 × 59"	Baltic birch
E	2	Top frame rail	¾ × 1½ × 59"	Birch
F	3	Top frame stile	¾ × 1½ × 18"	Birch
G	2	Cabinet divider	¾ × 1½ × 18¾"	Birch
H	1	Back spreader	¾ × 1½ × 58½"	Birch
I	1	Wall cleat	1½ × 3½ × 59"	2 × 4
J	1	Drawer bottom	½ × 11 × 18"	Plywood
K	2	Drawer end	½ × 11 × 6"	Plywood
L	2	Drawer side	½ × 17 × 6"	Plywood

HARDWARE

4 Self closing cup hinges for ½" stock

Bottom mount drawer slide (16")

2 10" × 2"-dia. brushed steel adjustable legs

4 Brushed steel door pulls

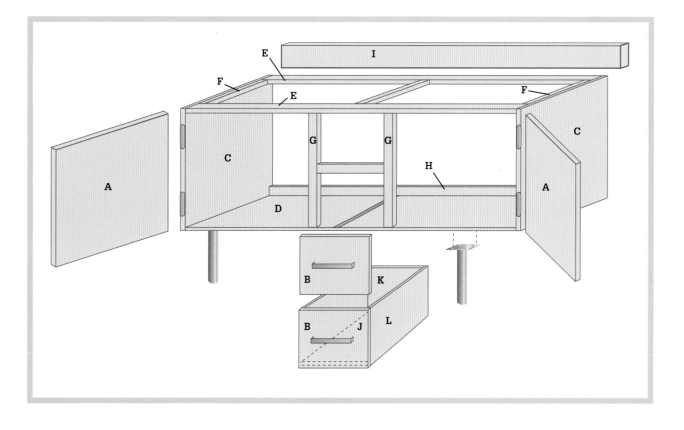

Baltic birch is considered the premier cabinetry plywood because of its extremely attractive and consistent surface patterns, and its uniform edge appearance that can eliminate the need for additional edge treatments such as wood veneer tape. This type of plywood features voidless plies, so that the layers have no visual gaps along the edges. The facing takes stain well, but most people choose to use a clear finish such as polyurethane to allow the beauty of the wood to come through. If you're determining the measurements for your own vanity cabinet, be aware that Baltic birch plywood usually comes in 5 × 5-ft. sheets, as opposed to the standard 4 × 8-ft. sheets.

How to Build a Custom Vanity Cabinet

Cut the pieces for the top frame from solid ½" birch—two 59" rails and three 18" stiles. Use a pocket jig to drill two pocket holes at each end of the stiles, and then glue and screw them to the rails with pocket screws.

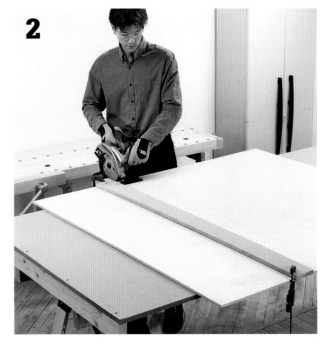

Cut the side and bottom panels, and door and drawer fronts, from a single sheet of Baltic birch plywood. Use a circular saw equipped with a sharp, thin-kerf ripping blade. Use a straightedge guide and saw the panels with the good side facing down.

3

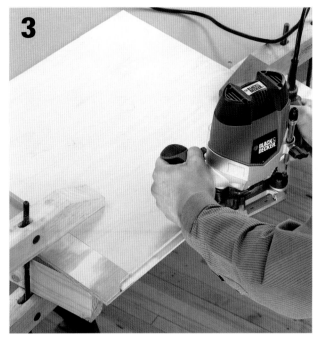

Cut rabbets for the bottom panel in the bottom inside edges of the both side panels. Use a router fitted with a ½" piloted rabbeting bit, set to ¼" depth. Sand as necessary to clean and smooth the rabbets.

4

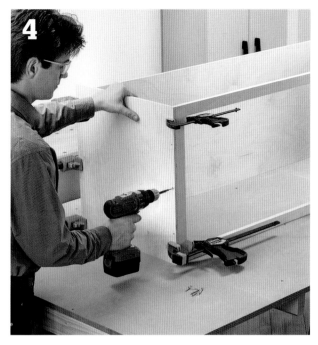

Assemble the cabinet case by gluing and clamping the end panels to the bottom panel. Glue and clamp the top frame into position between the tops of the end panels. Screw the end panels into the top frame with two 2" wood screws on either side. Secure the bottom panel in place with finishing nails through end panels into the bottom panel.

5

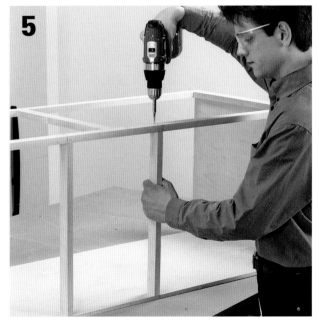

Cut and position solid birch dividers between the bottom panel and top frame. Measure to ensure the dividers are in correct position, check for level, then screw the bottom panel and top frame to the dividers. Add a central divider between the vertical dividers to create a visual backing for the gap between the drawer fronts.

6

Attach legs to the bottom of the cabinet case, inset about 2" from front corners. Secure the legs according to manufacturer's directions. The 10" metal legs here were screwed onto a bolt projecting through a hole in the bottom panel. The bolt is attached to a mounting plate screwed to the bottom of the bottom panel.

(continued)

7

Position the cabinet in place, check for level, and measure from the floor to the bottom edge of the top frame. Mark that line and screw a 2 × 4 cleat to wall with 3½" lag screws, keeping the top of the cleat aligned with the mark.

8

Position the cabinet so that the top frame rests on the wall cleat. Check level and shim as necessary, then nail finish nails through the end panels into the ends of the wall cleat. Adjust the front feet according to manufacturer's directions so that the cabinet is level.

9

Cut the spreader for the rear of the cabinet and place it on top of bottom panel, between the two side panels. Nail the spreader in place with finish nails, nailed through the end panels into the ends of the spreader.

10

Cut the sides, back, and bottom panels for the drawer box. Glue and clamp the pieces together, and edge nail them together with brads to reinforce the drawer box. Attach slides to the bottom of the drawer and the bottom of the cabinet in the drawer opening.

Sand the edges of the drawer and door fronts, working from about 100 grit down to 180 grit. **Note:** If you aren't satisfied with the look of the drawer and door edges, use filler before sanding to ensure they are absolutely smooth, or cover the edges with wood veneer tape prior to finishing the cabinet.

Mount the cabinet doors using adjustable cup hinges. Check that the doors are mounted square and plumb, adjusting the hinges as necessary.

Clamp the drawer front into place on the divider. Drill pilot holes and attach the drawer front with four No. 8 × ¾" panhead screws. Check that the drawer slides in and out freely. Screw 1 × cleats for the top drawer (false) front onto the inside faces of dividers. Screw through the cleats into the back of the drawer front to secure it in place.

Sink nailheads and cover exposed nail and screwheads with stainable wood putty. Sand the putty smooth and apply your finish of choice. We finished the cabinet with a brush-on stain, but use clear polyurethane if you prefer the natural look of the birch. Mark positions of drawer pulls, drill mounting holes, and install pulls.

Double-Bowl Vanity Top

Side-by-side double sinks are a wonderful addition to bathrooms large enough to accommodate the extra fixture. Often called "his-and-her" sinks, double sinks can be indispensable in a busy bathroom serving a large household, or for a couple whose schedules put them in the master bath at the same time each day.

The first issue to consider in adding a double sink is available space. You need to maintain the minimum required space around the sink, including 30 inches of clear space in front of the sink (but no less than 21 inches) and 30 inches from the center of one sink to the center of the other. Any sink or vanity edge should be at least 4 inches from a side wall, and should not impede door swing.

You'll also want to decide how much plumbing modification you're willing to do. Side-by-side standalone sinks, such as pedestals or wall-mounted models, require new supply and drains. But a double sink vanity like the one shown here can be added simply by using dual-use hardware that splits the existing supply and drain lines.

Tools & Materials ▸

Carpenter's level	Silicone caulk
Screwdrivers	Dual outlet valves
Power drill	Braided steel supply
Basin wrench	lines
Stud finder	P-trap
Adjustable wrench	PVC connections
Hacksaw	Plumber's putty

A double-bowl vanity is a useful fixture for accommodating multiple users during rush hour in your bathroom. Most home centers stock a selection of double-bowl options, but for the best variety allow enough time for a custom order (usually 1 to 6 weeks).

Double Drains

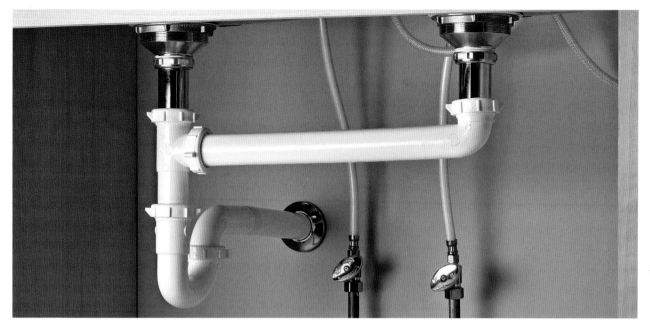

Double-bowl vanities are plumbed very similar to double-bowl kitchen sinks. In most cases, the drain tailpieces are connected beneath one of the tailpieces at a continuous waste T. The drain line from the second bowl must slope downward toward the T. From the T, the drain should have a trap (usually a P-trap) that connects to the trap arm coming out of the wall.

Drain in Floor

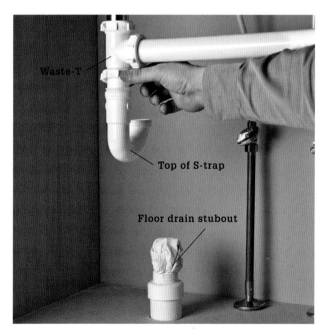

If your drain stubout comes up out of the floor instead of the wall, you'll need an S-trap to tie into it instead of a P-trap. Attach one half of the S-trap to the threaded bottom of the waste-T.

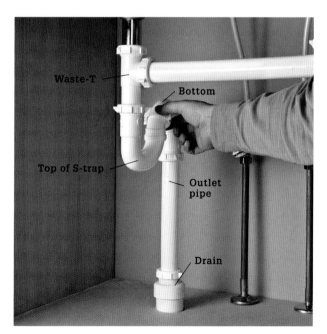

Attach the other half of the S-trap to the stubout with a slip fitting. This should result in the new fitting facing downward. Join the halves of the S-trap together with a slip nut, trimming the unthreaded end if necessary.

How to Install a Double Sink and Vanity

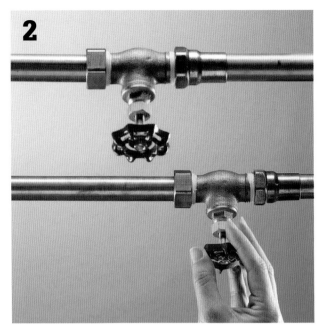

Shut off the supply valves located under the sink. Disconnect and remove the supply lines connecting the faucet to the valves. Loosen the P-trap nuts at both ends and remove the P-trap.

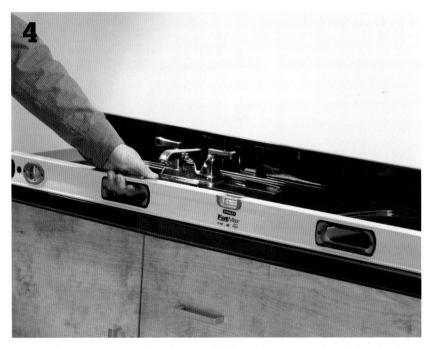

Remove the existing countertop and vanity. Turn off the water supply at the main shut-off valve. Drain remaining water by opening the faucet at the lowest point in the house. Use a hacksaw to remove the existing undersink shut-off valves.

Slide the new dual-outlet valve onto the hot water supply line, pass the nut and compression washer over the pipe, and tighten with a wrench. Install the dual-outlet valve on the cold water supply line in the same way.

Secure the new vanity in place by screwing it to the wall. Lay a bead of caulk along the underside and back edge of the countertop, where it will contact the vanity and wall. Set the countertop in place and check it for level. If your sinks are not integral, install them according to the type of sink you're using.

5

Seat the faucets for the double sinks as you would for a single sink, by applying a bead of putty on the underside of the bases (unless they are to be used with gaskets instead of putty). Secure them in place by tightening the locking nuts on the underside of the faucets.

6

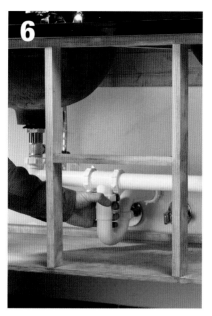

Connect a new PVC P-trap to the undersink drain pipe, and attach a T-connector to the trap. Extend PVC connections to the drain assemblies of both sinks.

7

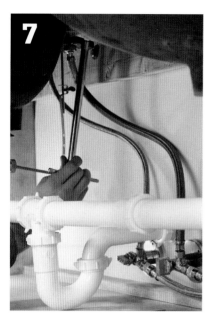

Connect the linkage for the pop-up drain stopper. Connect the braided steel cold water supply lines to the appropriate faucet tailpieces. Once the lines are secure, repeat for the hot water supply lines. Check that all connections are tightened securely.

8

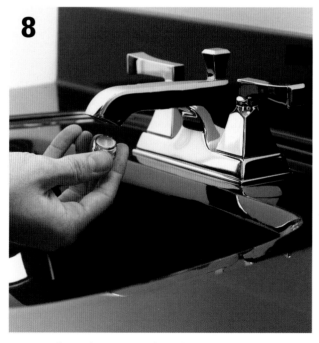

Turn on the main water supply and then turn on the water supply to the faucets. Remove the faucet aerators and run water in the sinks to check the supply lines and drain connections for leaks. Tighten the connections if you find any, and replace the aerators.

Leak Finder ▶

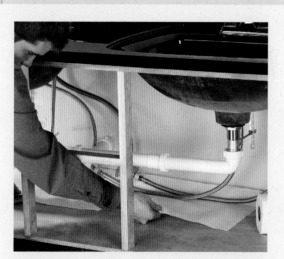

To quickly and easily find an undersink leak, lay bright white pieces of paper, or paper towels, under the pipes and drain connections. Open the water supply valves and run water in the sinks. It should be clear exactly where the water dripped from by the location of any drips on the paper.

COUNTERTOPS

Choosing countertops for your kitchen, bathroom, or even a workspace like a laundry room is an exercise in sifting through an embarrassment of riches. The number of countertop materials continues to grow, and the variations in appearance are almost too many to count.

So finding the right countertops for your space and life is, like selecting cabinets, a matter of balancing the look you prefer, the performance you need, and the cost you can afford.

The best countertops hold up to day-to-day abuse without scarring, chipping, or otherwise degrading. This may be less of concern if you're adding a countertop to a vanity in a guest bathroom, and will be top of mind if you're seeking out new countertops for a busy kitchen. Solid-surface materials, natural stone, and some recycled countertop materials will all provide durable surfaces that will take a lot of punishment without looking any worse for the wear.

Of course, these materials all vary widely in cost, which may be the deciding factor. There's no denying the unmatched beauty of natural marble or granite, but they'll set you back a pretty penny if you're looking to cover all the base cabinets in a large kitchen. Fortunately, you can find the look of those stones mimicked in engineered and laminate countertops for significantly less cost.

Lastly, you'll also need to decide if you want to install your own countertops. Some materials, such as solid-surface quartz countertops, should ideally be installed by qualified professionals, while others— such as post-form or tile counters—can easily be installed by anyone with even modest DIY skills.

Countertop Basics

Finding the perfect countertop is a matter of honing down all the possibilities to determine the one that best meets your needs and tastes. It all boils down to the look you want, how durable the surface needs to be, and your budget. Start with the amount you're willing to spend because it will likely narrow your choices quite a bit.

Three factors will affect the final cost of any countertop: the actual cost of the material, the cost of fabrication, and any special features. The most expensive countertops are natural stone, reflecting how difficult it is to quarry and process the material. The look is considered the epitome of luxury, which is why the surface appearances of stones from marble to slate are reproduced in a variety of other countertops, from engineered stone to laminates.

Engineered stone, quartz, and solid-surface countertops are the next step down in terms of cost. They are handsome, durable surfaces known for sophisticated looks. But like stone, most of these require professional installation—which means adding the cost of fabrication to the final bill.

Wood, concrete, recycled materials, and metal countertops or cheaper still, and in most cases you can choose to do the installation yourself, saving quite a bit on the final cost of the countertop. Laminates are the least expensive option and fairly simple for the home DIYer to install.

But even if you're considering more expensive options, you can save a little money by forgoing features like ogee or other profiled edges and special fixtures that require extensive countertop modification. Another cost-saving strategy is to use premium surfaces on an island or other small area of a larger room, using a less-expensive option over the

A recycled glass countertop can be a sophisticated look in the right kitchen, and offers a durable, long-lasting countertop surface at a reasonable price. You will, however, need to have the countertop professionally installed.

larger area. For instance, it has become a trend to use marble or granite on a centerpiece island, with quartz or laminate on the other countertops in the kitchen. Lastly, if you're having professionals fabricate and install your countertop, insist that they do the original measurements as well—that way any errors in fabrication come off their bottom line, rather than adding to your bill.

Sink Story ▶

Whether you're choosing kitchen counters or a new top for your bathroom vanities, chances are good that the countertop will need to be paired with a sink. The type of sink you already own or want to purchase may affect your choice of countertop. In general, self-rimming sinks will work with just about any countertop. But other sinks will only work with certain types of counters. For instance, if you're determined to use an undermount sink, you won't be able to use a post-form counter because the edges need to be waterproof. Likewise, the counter may influence sink selection. Some solid-surface materials can be fabricated with integrated sinks and even integrated backsplashes. The point is, countertop selection and choosing a sink go hand in glove, and should be done at the same time to head off potential problems.

Design Considerations

As much as budget will play a part in the countertop material you choose, you'll still have a diversity of looks to choose from. You'll be selecting from among different colors, patterns, and even textures.

Colors, in particular, are a growing piece of the puzzle. There has never been a bigger selection of countertop colors available. You can certainly lean toward more traditional and "safe" grays, blacks, whites, and off-whites. You'll find those hues in every material offered. But you also find a full palette of other colors, in shades from subtle to bold. Recycled glass countertops include dynamic options that allow you to integrate flecks of royal blue or shiny fire-engine red into your kitchen design. Recycled paper countertops are offered in dusky colors that can lend a bit of drama to an otherwise understated room. Solid surface and laminate manufacturers now offer a head-spinning selection of colors that seem to be nearly limitless—with the potential to custom order even more unusual colors. A few products, such as the enameled volcanic rock countertop Pyrolave, provide deep, vibrant pulse-quickening blues, reds, and yellows that reward the daring homeowner with a one-of-a-kind look.

Patterns are nearly as varied. The swirls of marble and flecks of granite are reproduced in laminate and solid-surface countertops, and you'll also find striations, repetitive patterns, and more. Textural options are naturally more limited by practicality. Although the vast majority of countertops are still smooth, glossy surfaces, you can find matte and even pebbled textures if you're so inclined.

Where countertops are concerned, design cannot be separated from function. If you are an avid cook, it may make sense to spend a bit more on a durable and heat-resistant counter such as granite, and avoid those prone to showing wear and tear, such as traditional butcher block or ceramic tile. Natural stone countertops are going to be some of the most durable, but many require regular maintenance, such as a yearly resealing. Whenever you're considering these surfaces, inquire about upkeep. Solid-surface counters, including quartz, engineered stone, and surfaces such as Corian®, are all durable, tolerate hot pans and resist scratching well.

The elegant countertops in this modest kitchen are just one of the many faces of the solid-surface material Corian®, a fairly inexpensive option that must be professionally installed, but that is incredibly durable.

There are ways to save money even on high-end countertops. Although these counters appear to be solid granite, they are actually granite shells clad over a subsurface—considerably less expensive than solid granite counters, but no less durable.

Countertop Materials

Choose a countertop material that fits your budget, but also make your selection based on how you'll use the surface and the look that appeals to you.

- **Natural stone.** This broad category includes expensive luxury surfaces that can transform a kitchen into a showcase. These are some of the priciest countertop options, but any natural stone surfaces are likely to last the life of the house and just as unlikely to ever go out of style. Different quarry stones can display remarkably different appearances. Marble is the most expensive natural stone and truly distinctive with its enticing veining and rich whites, grays, blacks, and even reds and greens. Granite is the most popular natural stone both for its attractive flecks and colorations, and for the naturally wear-and-tear-resistant surface (it's the hardest of countertop stones). Both marble and granite should be resealed once a year or more to prevent staining and discoloration. Soapstone has been used in kitchens for centuries; it's easy to work with and resists stains and other damage and can be oiled to an attractive finish. Slate is durable, hard, and dense. Scratches can be rubbed out and the surface does not need to be sealed. Slate also comes in appealing shades of green, purple, gray, and black, and even the rare red.

- **Laminate.** Although laminate countertops are still manufactured in the same way—layers of resin-soaked papers and plastic are bonded together under extreme pressure to form a waterproof material—today's laminate countertops come in an incredible range of looks featuring different colors, patterns, and even textures. And though you'll still have to contend with seams, they are subtler than ever before. Some laminate manufacturers even offer countertops with color that runs completely through the surface. These are pricier versions; the greater selection is represented by the "post-form" counters widely available at home centers in various lengths and styles. The surfaces are, in any case, more susceptible to heat damage and scratching than other countertop options.

- **Solid-surface.** Fabricated from a mixture of organic (usually stone chips) and inorganic additives, solid-surface countertops such as Corian® are made and installed without seam lines, and colored throughout so that scratches can be sanded or buffed out. They shouldn't be subjected to hot plates or used as cutting boards, but are otherwise sturdy and durable. Solid-surface materials are available in an amazing

Marble is a timeless choice for any kitchen, one that is the height of style and nearly indestructible.

Waterproof, durable, and easy to install, a countertop like this Corian® double sink vanity counter is also attractive and unique.

range of colors and patterns, and custom features such as drain boards and integral sinks can be fabricated into the countertop.

- **Recycled paper.** The newest type of countertops are made from recycled paper mixed with organic binders to create a solid surface that is the same color throughout. These are installed with a process similar to that used for other solid-surface countertops, and are considered a "green" option. The surface is waterproof, heat resistant, and scratch resistant. The cost is also on par with other solid-surface countertops, and the look is unusual and unique. The countertops can be fabricated with special edge treatments and features such as drain boards.

A recycled paper countertop like this can be crafted with built-in features like the drain board shown here.

- **Concrete.** This industrial material makes for a very durable countertop that is less expensive than natural stone and can be crafted to suit unusual shapes and layouts. Concrete can be dyed or stained just about any color you desire and features such as drain boards can be added

as part of the fabrication process. Any concrete countertop needs to be periodically resealed to prevent staining, and acidic foods can etch the surface. The countertop has to be carefully installed and correctly supported or any long span will be prone to cracking.

Ceramic tiles are a traditional choice for low-cost countertops that look handsome and are easy for the DIYer to install.

Stainless-steel countertops are a visually clean and striking look that blends well in a cook's kitchen full of stainless-steel appliances.

- **Tiles.** The most common type of tile countertop is ceramic, although natural stone and even metal tiles remain options in the middle of the price range. Stone tiles are a way to have the look of solid stone at far less cost—especially if you're willing and able to install the tiles. In any case, you'll always use floor rather than wall tiles because wall tiles won't stand up to the abuse most counters endure. The drawbacks to tile countertops are the grout lines that will inevitably get stained, and the fact that most tiles are very hard, which can lead to broken glassware and dinnerware.

- **Wood.** Butcher block is the most common wood countertop, made from thin slats of wood glued face to face. Butcher block countertops are easy to install, and other wood styles are not much harder. Today, you'll find all kind of hardwood and softwood countertops, each with it's own particular graining and look. Wood countertops can be finished light or dark, and sealed to inhibit the materials natural inclination to swell in the presence of moisture. Most wood countertops should not be used for cutting or as a resting place for hot pans, both of which can mar the surface.

- **Metals.** Stainless steel brings to mind professional kitchens, and zinc is more unusual and distinctive metal countertop choice that requires a good bit of upkeep. Stainless steel is the countertop of choice in restaurants, and the reasons professionals like stainless steel is that it doesn't stain and can handle the hottest pot you can throw at it. The metal is wrapped around and bonded to a substrate such as plywood during fabrication and installation—something that should be done by a professional. The one downside to this material—in addition to it being physically and visually cold—is that it shows fingerprints and watermarks. You can opt for matte or satin surfaces if this is a big concern.

- **Glass.** Recycled glass is a green countertop material offered in an astounding number of colors and surface appearances. The surface can look radically different, depending on the size and color of the glass fragments use, and the finished surface is heat and scratch resist and as durable as stone surfaces. Most of these countertops require professional installation and select carefully—bold colors may grow old long before the counter wears out. You can also have a cast-glass countertop made to your specifications, but be sure you love the material and the look; they are pricey and difficult to install or remove.

- **Quartz.** Quartz countertops resemble solid-surface countertops, but contain a higher percentage of mineral matter versus binders. Because all quartz surfaces are manufactured using essentially the same equipment and formulas, any differences between products is due to the type of quartz used. A quartz surface can't be scratched, is nonporous, is nonstaining, and doesn't need to be sealed. The surface can also withstand hot pots, and is hard as granite. It carries much of the attraction of granite and marble, at a lower price.

Recycled glass countertops come in a myriad of color blends, and single-color looks. All are unique, unusual and stunning.

A quartz countertop captures much of the beauty and durability of a stone countertop at a lower price.

Post-form Countertops

Post-form laminate countertops are available in stock and custom colors. Pre-mitered sections are available for two- or three-piece countertops that continue around corners. If the countertop has an exposed end, you will need an endcap kit that contains a pre-shaped strip of matching laminate. Post-form countertops have either a waterfall edge or a no-drip edge. Stock colors are typically available in 4-, 6-, 8-, 10-, and 12-foot straight lengths, and 6- and 8-foot mitered lengths.

Tools & Materials ▸

Tape measure	Belt sander
Framing square	Power drill and spade bit
Pencil	Cordless screwdriver
Straightedge	Post-form countertop
C-clamps	Wood shims
Hammer	Take-up bolts
Level	Drywall screws
Caulking gun	Wire brads
Jigsaw	Endcap laminate
Compass	Silicone caulk
Adjustable wrench	Wood glue

Post-form countertops are among the easiest and cheapest to install. They are a good choice for beginning DIYers, and the number of pattern and color options continues to grow.

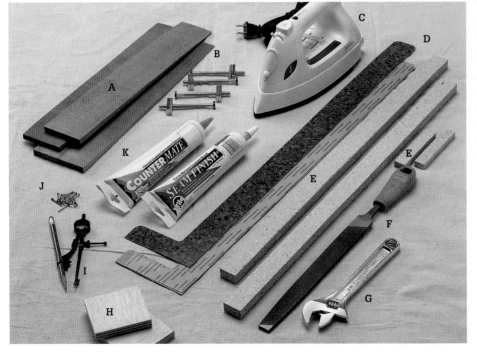

The following tools and materials will be used in this project: wood shims (A); take-up bolts for drawing miters together (B); household iron (C); endcap laminate to match countertop (D); endcap battens (E); file (F); adjustable wrench (G); buildup blocks (H); compass (I); fasteners (J); silicone caulk and sealer (K).

How to Install a Post-form Countertop

1

Option: Use a jigsaw fitted with a downstroke blade to cut post-form. If you are unable to locate a downstroke blade, you can try applying tape over the cutting lines, but you are still likely to get tear-out from a normal upstroke jigsaw blade.

2

Use a framing square to mark a cutting line on the bottom surface of the countertop. Cut off the countertop with a jigsaw using a clamped straightedge as a guide.

3

Attach the battens from the endcap kit to the edge of the countertop using carpenter's glue and small brads. Sand out any unevenness with a belt sander.

(continued)

4

Hold the endcap laminate against the end, slightly overlapping the edges. Activate the adhesive by pressing an iron set on medium heat against the endcap. Cool with a wet cloth, then file the endcap laminate flush with the edges of the countertop.

5

Position the countertop on the base cabinets. Make sure the front edge of the countertop is parallel to the cabinet faces. Check the countertop for level. Make sure that drawers and doors open and close freely. If needed, adjust the countertop with shims.

6

Because walls are usually uneven, use a compass to trace the wall outline onto the backsplash. Set the compass arms to match the widest gap, then move the compass along the length of the wall to transfer the outline to the top of the backsplash. Apply painter's tape to the top edge of the backsplash, following the scribed line (inset).

7

Remove the countertop. Use a belt sander to grind the backsplash to the scribe line.

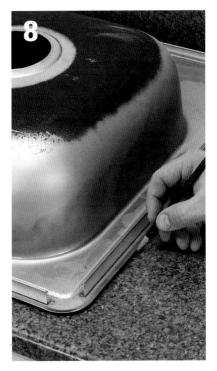

Mark the cutout for the self-rimming sink. Position the sink upside down on the countertop and trace its outline. Remove the sink and draw a cutting line ⅝" inside the sink outline.

Drill a starter hole just inside the cutting line. Make sink cutouts with a jigsaw. Support the cutout area from below so that the falling cutout does not damage the cabinet.

Apply a bead of silicone caulk to the edges of the mitered countertop sections. Force the countertop pieces tightly together.

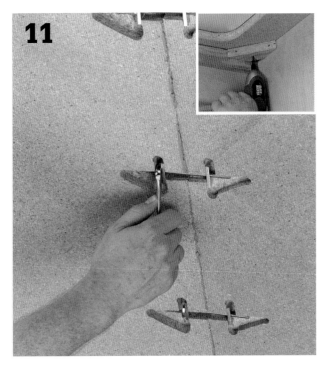

From underneath the countertop, install and tighten miter take-up bolts. Position the countertop tightly against the wall and fasten it to the cabinets by driving wallboard screws up through the corner brackets and into the countertop (inset). Screws should be long enough to provide maximum holding power, but not long enough to puncture the laminate surface.

Seal the seam between the backsplash and the wall with silicone caulk. Smooth the bead with a wet fingertip. Wipe away excess caulk.

Butcher Block Countertops

Butcher block slabs come in a variety of woods or—since they are made up of small pieces of wood glued together—a combination of different woods. They're available most commonly in maple or oak in end grain, which is composed of vertical pieces of wood, or edge grain and face grain, made up of long strips of wood. Making butcher block can be accomplished as an advanced DIY project, but it's often more cost-effective (and always faster) to purchase pieces in stock sizes and cut them down to fit your kitchen. Because butcher block is ideal for food prep areas but can be impractical near a sink or stove, another option is to install a small section of butcher block in combination with other countertop materials.

Tools & Materials ▸

Circular saw with cutting guide
Carpenter's square
Drill and bits
Bolt connector hardware
Caulk gun and silicone adhesive
Clamps
Sander
Varnish
Router with piloted roundover bit
Wood screws with fender washers
Jigsaw with downstroke bit
Brush and finish material
Tape
Connector fittings
Forstner bit
Silicone adhesive
Faucet and sink

Butcher block countertops enjoy continued popularity because of their natural beauty and warm wood tones.

Butcher block sold by the foot for countertop ranges from 1½" to 3" thick, although some end-grain products, used mostly for chopping blocks, can be up to 5" thick. For residential kitchens, the 1½"-thick material is the most available and most affordable choice. Stock length varies, but 6' and 12' slabs are common. You can also order the material with sink cutouts completed. Pre-made countertop is sold in the standard 25" depth, but wider versions (30" and 36") for islands are not difficult to find.

Butcher block countertop material comes pre-sealed, but a finish of varnish or oil, such as mineral or tung oil, is recommended. Seal cut wood around sink cutouts and on trimmed edges to keep it watertight.

A self-rimming sink is the easiest type to mount in a butcher block countertop, but undermount types can look stunning (just make sure to get a perfect seal on the end grain around the sink cutout).

End grain vs. face grain: Traditionally, butcher block countertop surfaces were made with square sections of wood (often maple) oriented with their end grain facing upward. This orientation creates a better, more

durable, knife-friendly cutting surface. For economy, many of today's butcher block sections are edge-glued with exposed edge grain or face grain.

Typical countertop material is 1½" wide and 25" deep, available in a number of lengths from 4' to 12' long.

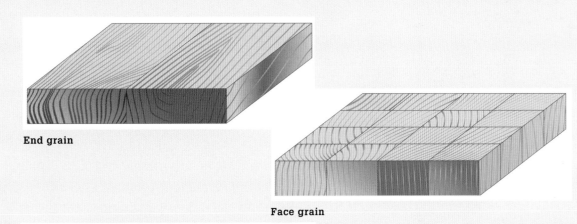

End grain

Face grain

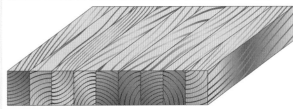

Edge grain

Butcher block that's constructed with the end grain oriented up is the most desirable, but it is relatively hard to find and fairly expensive. Material with the face grain or edge grain facing up is more common and more affordable.

How to Build a Butcher Block Countertop

1

2

Before beginning installation, allow the butcher block to acclimate to your home's moisture level for a couple of days. Wood contracts and expands with moisture and humidity, so it may have warped or expanded during transport. Place it level on the cabinet tops and let it sit until it's settled.

Measure your countertop area, adding 1" to the base cabinet depth to allow for overhang. Using a circular saw, cut the piece to size if needed. Butcher block with pre-cut miter corners and cutouts for kitchens is available, but if you're cutting the piece yourself, be sure to apply finish to each new raw edge.

3

4

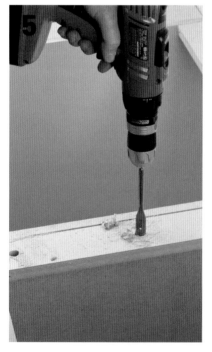

5

Butcher block should be attached using wood screws that allow for some movement. Mark three points in a line on the underside of the countertop, spacing rows of drilling points at 12-inch intervals.

Drill pilot holes for screws at drilling points. Stick tape to the bit 1" from the point to create a depth stop.

Drill corresponding holes in the cabinet base that are slotted or at least ⅜" larger than the screws you are using. When driven with a washer under the screw head, screws will be able to move slightly with the wood.

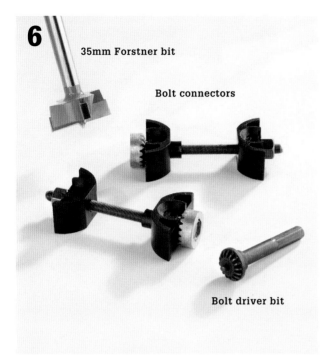

6

35mm Forstner bit

Bolt connectors

Bolt driver bit

Tip: In most cases butcher block countertops are not mitered at the corners as some other countertop types are. Instead, they are butted at the corners. You also may need to join two in-line pieces with a butt joint. In both instances, use connector fittings.

7

Make butt joints between countertop sections. Lay the two sections of countertop to be joined upside down on a flat work surface in their correct orientation. Mark drilling points for the connector holes. Drill the holes with a Forstner bit.

8

With the countertop sections roughly in position on the cabinets and flipped right-side up, apply a bead of silicone adhesive near the top of one mating edge.

9

From below, insert the connector bolt so the two heads are flat in the holes and then tighten the bolt with the driver bit (supplied with bolt hardware) to draw the two sections of countertop together. Do not overtighten.

(continued)

Clamp a piece of scrap wood to the end of the countertop so the tops are flush. The scrap wood prevents the router bit from rounding over the corner when the edge of the countertop is profiled.

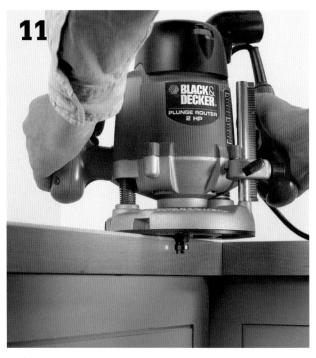

Pull the countertop section away from the wall a few inches and make a roundover cut along the front edges with a piloted roundover bit.

Attach the countertop to the cabinet mounting strips by driving screws up through the cabinet strips and into the countertop. The screws should be ¼" shorter than the distance from the bottom of the mounting strips to the top of the countertop. Use 1" fender washers with the screws and snug them up, but do not overtighten. Because of the counterbores and the washers, the countertop will be able to move slightly as it expands and contracts.

If installing a sink in your countertop, start by outlining the sink in the correct position as recommended in the installation material from the sink manufacturer. Mount a downstroke blade into the jigsaw (inset), and drill a starter hole just inside the sink outline. Make the cutout, taking care to stay just inside the cutting line. If you are installing an undermount sink, smooth the cuts up to the line with a power sander.

Variation: If you're installing an undermount sink, mark a centerpoint for drilling a hole to accommodate the faucet body following the recommendations of the faucet manufacturer. A 1⅜"-dia. hole is fairly standard.

14

Seal the edges of the sink opening with a varnish as instructed by the butcher block manufacturer, or by coating it generously with pure mineral oil or tung oil for a natural finish. Let sit for 15 minutes then wipe off the excess with a clean, lint-free cloth. Let it dry for 48 hours. Repeat six times, letting it dry thoroughly between coats.

15

Add the backsplash of your choice and caulk between the new countertop and the backsplash area with silicone caulk.

16

Install the faucet and sink and make the water supply and drain hookups.

Laminate Countertops

Building your own custom laminate countertop using sheets of plastic laminate and particleboard offers two advantages: the countertop you wind up will be less expensive than a custom-ordered countertop, and it may allow you more options in terms of colors and edge treatments. A countertop made with laminates also can be tailored to fit any space, unlike pre-made countertop material that is a standard width (usually 25").

Laminate is commonly sold in 8-ft. or 12-ft. lengths that are about $\frac{1}{20}$" thick. The lengths range from 30" strips to 48" sheets. The 30" strips are sized specifically for countertops, allowing for a 25"-wide countertop, a 1½"-wide front edge strip, and a short backsplash.

The plastic laminate is bonded to the particle-board or MDF substrate with contact cement, though most professional installers use products that are available only to the trades. Water-based contact cement is nonflammable and nontoxic, but solvent-based contact cement, which requires a respirator and is highly flammable, creates a much stronger, more durable bond.

Tools & Materials ▸

Tape measure	Router (with bevel
Framing square	cutting bit)
Straightedge	½" scrap wood
Scoring tool	¼" plywood
Paint roller	1 × 4 lumber
Bar clamps	¾" particleboard
Caulk gun	Sheet laminate
J-roller	Contact cement
Miter saw (as	Wood glue
needed)	¼" drywall screws
Compass	2" wallboard screws
Utility knife	Mineral spirits
Aviator snips	Wood filler
Circular saw	Finishing materials
Belt sander	Laminate
	Silicone caulk

Fabricating your own custom countertop from particleboard and plastic laminate is not exactly an easy DIY project, but it gives you unlimited options, and the results can be very satisfying.

Tips for Working with Laminate ▸

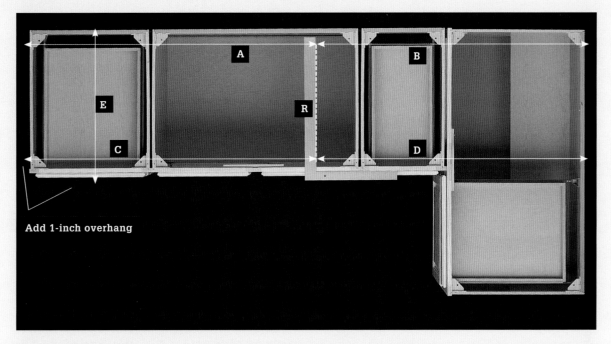

Add 1-inch overhang

Measure along the tops of the base cabinets to determine the size of the countertop. If the wall corners are not square, use a framing square to establish a reference line (R) near the middle of the base cabinets, perpendicular to the front of the cabinets. Take four measurements (A, B, C, D) from the reference line to the cabinet ends. Allow for overhangs by adding 1" to the length for each exposed end, and 1" to the width (E).

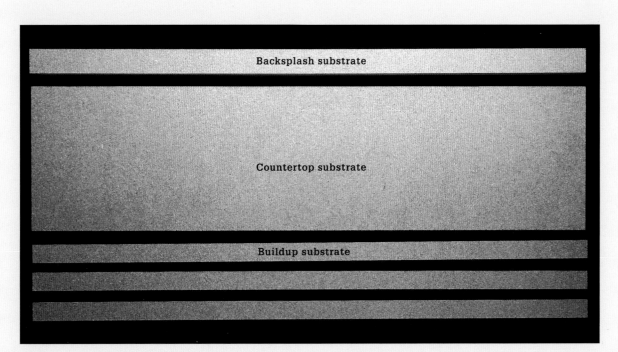

Backsplash substrate

Countertop substrate

Buildup substrate

Lay out cutting lines on the particleboard so you can rip-cut the substrate and buildup strips to size using a framing square to establish a reference line. Cut the core to size using a circular saw with a clamped straightedge as a guide. Cut 4" strips of particleboard for the backsplash and for joint support where sections of countertop core are butted together. Cut 3" strips for the edge buildups.

How to Build a Laminate Countertop

Join the countertop substrate pieces on the bottom side. Attach a 4" particleboard joint support across the seam using carpenter's glue and 1¼" wallboard screws.

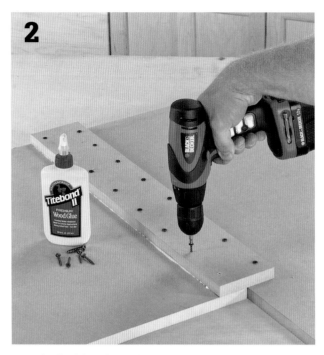

Attach 3"-wide edge build-up strips to the bottom of the countertop, using 1¼" wallboard screws. Fill any gaps on the outside edges with latex wood patch, and then sand the edges with a belt sander.

To determine the size of the laminate top, measure the countertop substrate. Laminate seams should not overlap the substrate. Add ½" trimming margin to both the length and width of each piece. Measure the laminate needed for face and edges of backsplash and for exposed edges of countertop substrate. Add ½" to each measurement.

Cut the laminate by scoring and then breaking it. Draw a cutting line, and then etch along the line with a utility knife or other sharp cutting tool. Use a straightedge as a guide. Making two passes with the scoring tool will help the laminate to break cleanly.

Bend the laminate toward the scored line until the sheet breaks cleanly. For better control on narrow pieces, clamp a straightedge along the scored line before bending the laminate. Wear gloves to avoid being cut by the sharp edges.

Option: Some laminate installers prefer to cut laminate with special snips that resemble aviator snips. Available from laminate suppliers, the snips are faster than scoring and snapping, and they are less likely to cause cracks or tears in the material. You'll still need to square the cut edges with a trimmer or router.

Create tight seams with plastic laminate by using a router and a straight bit to trim the edges that will butt together. Measure from the cutting edge of the bit to the edge of the router baseplate (A). Place the laminate on scrap wood and align the edges. To guide the router, clamp a straightedge on the laminate at distance A plus ¼", parallel to the laminate edge. Trim the laminate.

Apply laminate to the sides of the countertop first. Using a paint roller, apply two coats of contact cement to the edge of the countertop and one coat to the back of the laminate. Let the cement dry according to manufacturer's directions. Position the laminate carefully, and then press against the edge of the countertop. Bond the laminate to the countertop with a J-roller.

(continued)

Use a router and a flush-cutting bit to trim the edge strip flush with top and bottom surfaces of the countertop substrate. At edges where the router cannot reach, trim the excess laminate with a file. Apply the laminate to the remaining edges, and trim with the router.

Test-fit the laminate top on the countertop substrate. Check that the laminate overhangs all the edges. At seam locations, draw a reference line on the core where the laminate edges will butt together. Remove the laminate. Make sure all the surfaces are free of dust, and then apply one coat of contact cement to the back of the laminate and two coats to the substrate. Place spacers made of ½"-thick scrap wood at 6" intervals across the countertop core. Because contact cement bonds instantly, spacers allow the laminate to be positioned accurately over the core without bonding. Align the laminate with the seam reference line. Beginning at one end, remove the spacers and press the laminate to the countertop core.

Apply contact cement to the remaining substrate and the next piece of laminate. Let the cement dry, and then position the laminate on the spacers and carefully align the butt seam. Beginning at the seam edge, remove the spacers and press the laminate to the countertop substrate.

Roll the entire surface with a J-roller to bond the laminate to the substrate. Clean off any excess contact cement with a soft cloth and mineral spirits.

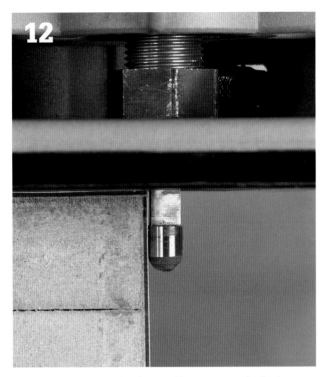

12

Remove the excess laminate with a router and a flush-cutting bit. At edges where the router cannot reach, trim the excess laminate with a file. The countertop is now ready for the final trimming with a bevel-cutting bit.

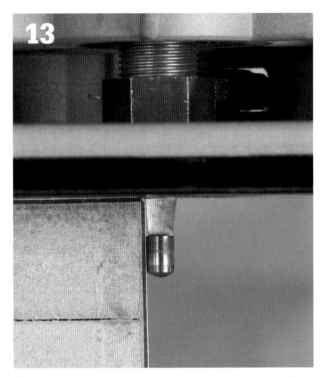

13

Finish-trim the edges with a router and a 15° bevel-cutting bit. Set the bit depth so that the bevel edge is cut only on the top laminate layer. The bit should not cut into the vertical edge surface.

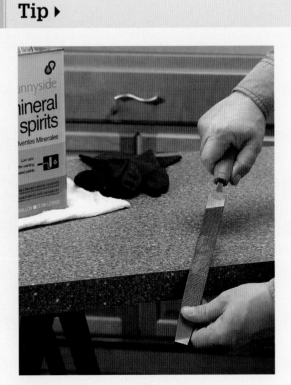

Tip ▶

File all the edges smooth. Use downward file strokes to avoid chipping the laminate.

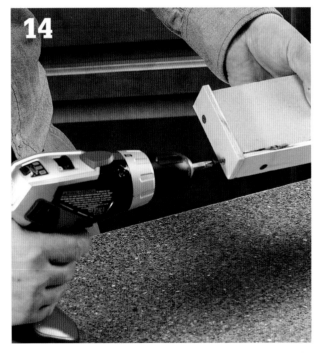

14

Cut 1¼"-wide strips of ¼" plywood to form an overhanging scribing strip for the backsplash. Attach it to the top and sides of the backsplash substrate with glue and wallboard screws. Cut laminate pieces and apply to the exposed sides, top, and front of the backsplash. Trim each piece as it is applied.

(continued)

15

Test-fit the countertop and backsplash. Because your walls may be uneven, use a compass to trace the wall outline onto the backsplash-scribing strip. Use a belt sander to grind the backsplash to the scribe line.

16

Apply a bead of silicone caulk to the bottom edge of the backsplash.

17

Position the backsplash on the countertop, and clamp it into place with bar clamps. Wipe away the excess caulk, and let it dry completely.

18

Screw 2" wallboard screws through the countertop and into the backsplash core. Make sure the screw heads are countersunk completely for a tight fit against the base cabinet. Install the countertops.

Repairing and Maintaining Laminate ▶

Laminate countertops can be found in more kitchens than any other type of countertop material. The main reason is that laminate is versatile and inexpensive. It's stain resistant, durable, sanitary, and it's the only material that requires no maintenance aside from regular cleaning (you can't say that about even the most expensive marble or stainless-steel surfaces). If you like the look of laminate, its only real drawbacks are that it's susceptible to damage.

Topping the list of common laminate damage problems are knife marks, burns, delamination, and misaligned or curling seams. Although damaged laminate cannot be easily repaired and scars cannot be removed, there are some simple repairs you can make to spruce up your laminate.

Did someone forget to use a cutting board? You can help hide scratches and light gouges in laminate with a commercial seam filler, available from laminate manufacturers. For chips or small holes, you can purchase a repair kit from home and hardware stores. Seam filler and repair kits consist of a plastic compound that you mix to match the color of your surface. Follow the product directions for mixing and applying the patch. Again, the repair won't be invisible, but it's better than doing nothing.

Burn marks are next on the list, as many a laminate countertop has been marred by a hot pan, a fallen cigarette, or a potholder left too close to a stovetop burner. If the burn is near a cooking area, you're in luck: you can cut out the damage and set a large tile into the surface to create a built-in trivet.

A vinyl and leather repair kit can be used to make touch-up repairs on laminate countertops. To use this kit, prepare the repair area with an abrasive pad, blend paints to achieve similar color, apply the paint to the repair area, cover with a clear coat, and then heat-set with a household iron after the paint dries.

Seam-filling compound is purchased pretinted to match common plastic laminate colors. It can be used to repair minor chips and scratches or to fill separated seams between laminate sheets.

Use a J-roller to rebond loose or bubbled laminate to its substrate. Heat the repair area with an iron first.

Concrete Countertop

Cast concrete countertops have many unique characteristics. They are durable, heat resistant, and relatively inexpensive (if you make them yourself). But most of all, they are highly attractive and a great fit in contemporary kitchens or bathrooms.

A concrete countertop may be cast in place or formed offsite and installed like a natural stone countertop. Casting offsite makes more sense for most homeowners. In addition to keeping the mess and dust out of your living spaces, working in a garage or even outdoors lets you cast the countertops with the finished surface face down in the form. This way, if you do a careful job building the form, you can keep the grinding and polishing to a bare minimum. In some cases, you may even be able to simply remove the countertop from the form, flip it over, and install it essentially as is.

Tools & Materials ▶

Tape measure
Pencil
Circular saw
Jigsaw
Power drill and right-
angle drill guide
Level
Carpenter's square
Reciprocating saw
Aviation snips
2" coarse drywall
screws
Deck screws (3, 3½")

Wire mesh
Pliers
Concrete mixer
5-gal. buckets
Shovel
Wheelbarrow
Wooden float
Angle grinder
Belt sander
Automotive buffer
Insulation board
Plastic sheeting
Rubber mallet

Black or colored
silicone caulk
Grinding and polishing
pads
Melamine-coated
particleboard
Concrete sealer
Coloring agent
Compass
No. 3 rebar
Tie wire
Panel or silicone
adhesive

Bagged concrete mix
Paste wax
Work gloves and eye
protection

If installing sink:
Knockout for faucet
Buffing bonnet
Faucet set
Sink
Polyurethane varnish

Building a custom concrete countertop like this is an easier project than you might think. All of the building materials and techniques are covered in this project.

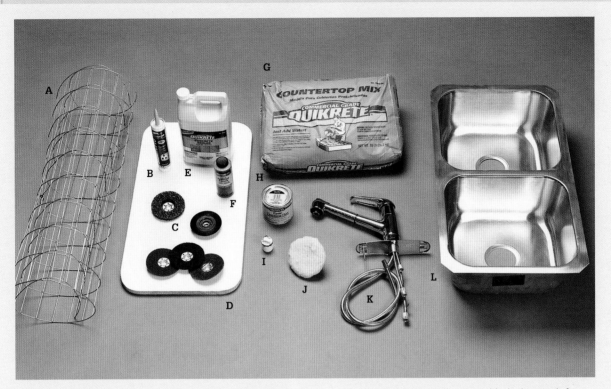

The basic supplies needed to build your countertop form and cast the countertop include: (A) welded wire mesh for reinforcement; (B) black or colored silicone caulk; (C) grinding and polishing pads; (D) melamine-coated particleboard for constructing the form; (E) concrete sealer; (F) coloring agent (liquid or powder); (G) bagged concrete countertop mix or high/early mix rated for 5,000 psi; (H) paste wax; (I) knockout for faucet, if installing sink; (J) buffing bonnet for polisher; (K) faucet set; and (L) sink.

Custom Features: Concrete countertops are normally cast as flat slabs, but if you are willing to put a little more time and effort into it, there are many additional features you can create during the pour. A typical 3"-tall backsplash is challenging, but if you have room behind the faucet you can create a ¾"-tall backsplash shelf in the backsplash area. Or, if you search around for some additional information, you can learn how to cast a drain board directly into the countertop surface. And there is practically no end to the decorative touches you can apply using pigments and inserts.

Estimating Concrete for Countertops: After you design your project and determine the actual dimensions, you'll need to estimate the amount of concrete you'll need. Concrete is measured by volume, in cubic feet; multiply the length by the width and then by the thickness of the finished countertop for volume in cubic inches, then divide the sum by 1,728 for cubic feet. For example,

a countertop that will be 48" long × 24" deep × 3½" thick will require 2⅓ cu. ft. of mixed concrete (48 × 24 × 3.5 / 1,728 = 2⅓) or four 80-lb. bags of countertop mix.

Countertop mix is specially formulated concrete designed for use in either pre-cast or cast-in-place projects. Countertop mix contains additives that improve the workability, strength, and finish of the mix.

How to Cast a Concrete Countertop

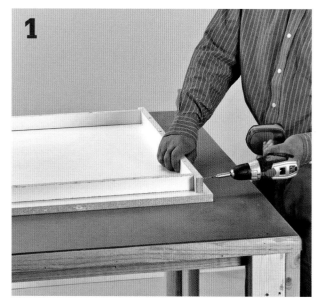

Cut 1½"-wide strips of ¾" melamine-coated particleboard for the form sides. Cut the strips to length (26 and 81½" as shown here) and drill two countersunk pilot holes ⅜" in from the ends of the front and back form sides. Assemble the strips into a frame by driving a 2" drywall screws at each pilot hole and into the mating ends of the end form strips.

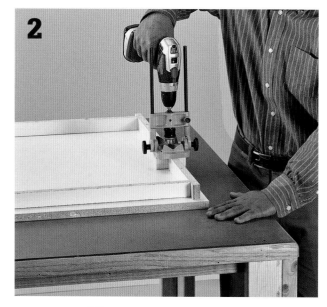

Use a power drill mounted in a right-angle drill guide to drill ¼"-dia. guide holes for 3" deck screws at 6" intervals all the way through the tops of the form sides. Countersink the holes so the screw heads will be recessed slightly below the surface.

With the base melamine-side up, center the melamine-strip frame pieces on the base. Check the corners with a carpenter's square to make sure they're square. Drive one 3½" deck screw per form side near the middle. The screwheads should be slightly below the top edges of the forms. Check for square again, and continue driving the 3½" screws at 6" intervals through the pilot holes. Check for square frequently. **Note:** Do not drive any screws up through the underside of the form base—you won't be able to lift the countertop and access the screws when it's time to strip off the forms.

Make the sink knockout blanks by stacking two pieces of ¾" melamine. The undermount sink we used requires a 20 × 31" knockout with corners that are rounded at a 2" radius. Cut two pieces of ¾"-thick MDF to 20 × 31" square using a table saw. With a compass, mark 2"-radius curves at each corner for trimming. Make the trim cuts with a jigsaw. Cut just outside the trim line and sand up to it with a pad sander for a smooth curve.

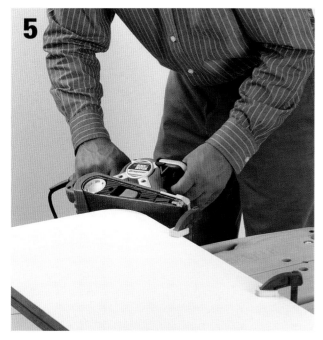

Clamp the two pieces of melamine face-to-face for the knockout and gang-sand the edges and corners so that they're smooth and even. Use a belt sander on a stationary table or an oscillating spindle sander. Don't oversand or the sink knockout will be too small.

Because gluing the faces together can add height to the knockout (and cause the concrete finishing tools to bang into it when they ride on the form tops), attach each blank directly to the layer below it using countersunk screws. Keep the edges aligned perfectly, especially if you're planning to install an undermount sink.

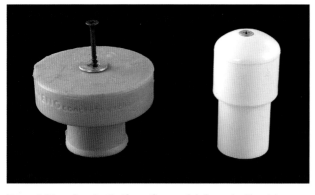

Faucet Knockouts Option: If your sink faucet will not be mounted on the sink deck, you'll need to add a knockout to your form for the faucet hole (best to choose a single-handle faucet), according to the requirements of the manufacturer. You can order knockouts from a concrete countertop supplies distributor, or you can create them with PVC pipe that has an outside diameter equal to the required faucet hole size. To anchor the PVC knockout, cover one end with a flat cap made for that size tubing. Drill a guide hole through the center of the cap so you can secure it with a screw. The top of the cap should be exactly flush with the form sides once it is installed. Before securing, position the knockout next to a form side and compare the heights. If the knockout is taller, file or sand the uncapped end so their lengths match.

Seal exposed edges of the sink knockout with fast-drying polyurethane varnish, and then caulk the form once the varnish is dry. Run a very thin bead of colored silicone caulk (the coloring allows you to see where the caulk has been laid on the white melamine) in all the seams and then smooth carefully with your fingertip. In addition to keeping the wet concrete from seeping into gaps in the form, the caulk will create a slight roundover on the edges of the concrete. Caulk around the bottoms of the knockouts as well.

(continued)

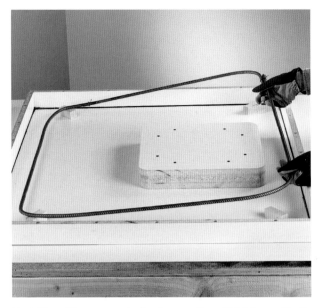

Variation: If your countertop is more than 2" thick, use No. 3 rebar (⅜" dia.) for the primary reinforcement. Do not use rebar on thinner countertops because the rebar will be too close to the surface and can telegraph through. Bend the rebar to fit around the perimeter of the form using a rebar or conduit bender. The rebar needs to be at least 1" away from all edges (including knockouts) and 1" away from the top surface. Tie the ends of the rebar with wire and set it in the form on temporary 1" spacers.

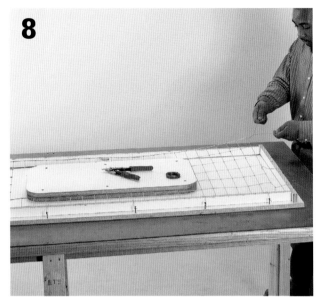

8

Cut a piece of welded wire (also called rewire) in a 4 × 4" grid so it's 2" smaller than the interior form dimensions. Make a cutout for the sink and faucet knockouts, making sure the rewire does not come closer than 1" to any edge, surface, or knockout. Flatten it as best you can and then hang it with wires that are attached to the tops of the forms with screws (you'll remove the screws and cut the wires after the concrete is placed).

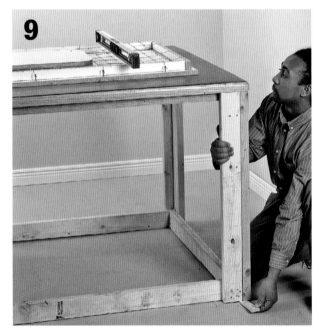

9

Clamp or screw the base of the form to a sturdy workbench or table so it can't move during finishing and curing. Check for level and insert shims between the worktop and the benchtop if needed for leveling. If you're concerned about mess, slip a sheet of 3-mil plastic on the floor under the workbench.

10

Blend water with liquid cement color (if desired) in a 5-gal. bucket prior to adding to the mixer.

11

12

Slowly pour concrete countertop mix into the mixer and blend for a minimum of 5 minutes. Properly mixed material will flow easily into molds. Add small amounts of water as necessary to achieve the desired consistency.

Fill the countertop form, making sure to pack the concrete into corners and press it through the reinforcement. Overfill the form slightly.

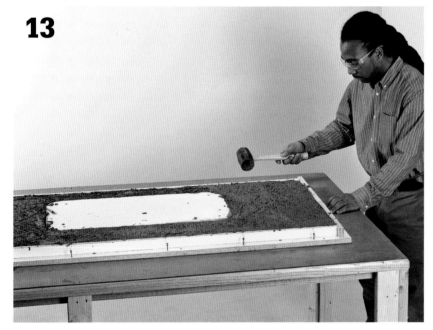

13

14

Vibrate the form vigorously as you work to settle concrete into all the voids. You can rent a concrete vibrator for this purpose, or simply strike the form repeatedly with a rubber mallet. If you have a helper and a sturdy floor and worktable, lift up and down on the ends of the table, bouncing it to cause vibrations. Make sure the table remains level when you're through.

Strike off excess concrete from the form using a 2 x 4 drawn along the tops of the forms in a sawing motion. If voids are created, pack them with fresh concrete and restrike. Do not overwork the concrete.

(continued)

Snip the wire ties holding the rewire mesh once you are certain you won't need to vibrate the form any further. Embed the cut ends attached to the rewire below the concrete surface.

Smooth the surface of the concrete with a screed, such as a length of angle iron or square metal tubing. Work slowly with a sawing motion, allowing the bleed water to fill in behind the screed. Since this surface will be the underside of the countertop, no further tooling is required. Cover the concrete with plastic and let dry undisturbed for three to five days.

Remove the plastic covering and remove the forms. Do not pry against the fresh concrete. In most cases, you'll need to cut apart the sink knockout to prevent damaging the countertop when removing it. Drill a starter hole and then carefully cut up to the edge of the knockout. Cut the knockout into chunks until you can remove it all. The edges of the concrete will be fragile, so be very careful.

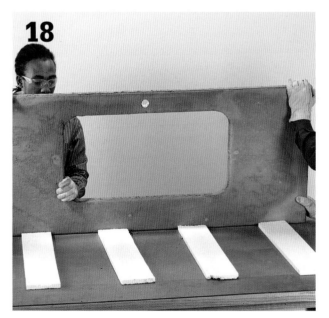

Flip the countertop so the finished surface is exposed (you'll need a helper or two). Be extremely careful. The best technique is to roll the countertop onto an edge, position several shock-absorbing sleepers beneath it (rigid insulation board works very well), and then gently lower the countertop onto the sleepers.

19

Grind the countertop surface with a series of increasingly fine grinding pads mounted on a shock-protected 5" angle grinder (variable speed). This is messy work and can require hours to get the desired result. Rinse the surface regularly with clean water and make sure it stays wet during grinding. For a gleaming surface, mount still finer pads (up to 1,500 grit) on the grinder and wet-polish.

20

Clean and seal the concrete with several coats of quality concrete sealer (one with penetrating and film-forming agents). For extra protection and a renewable finish, apply a coat of paste wax after the last coat of sealer dries.

21

Mount the sink (if undermount). Sinks are easier to install prior to attaching the countertop on the cabinet. Attach the sink according to the manufacturer's directions. Undermount sinks like this are installed with undermount clips and silicone adhesive. Self-rimming sinks likely will require some modifications to the mounting hardware (or at least you'll need to buy some extra-long screws) to accommodate the thickness of the countertop.

22

Make sure the cabinet is adequately reinforced and that as much plumbing as possible has been done, and apply a thick bead of silicone adhesive to the tops of the cabinets and stretchers. With at least one helper, lower the countertop onto the base and position it where you wish. Let the adhesive dry overnight before completing the sink and faucet hookups.

Tile Countertops

Ceramic and porcelain tiles remain suitable choices for countertops and backsplashes for a number of reasons: they're available in a vast range of sizes, styles, and colors; they're durable and repairable; and many tiles are reasonably priced. With careful planning, tile is also easy to install, making a custom countertop a good do-it-yourself project.

The best tile for most countertops is glazed ceramic or porcelain floor tile. Glazed tile is better than unglazed because of its stain resistance, and floor tile is better than wall tile because it's thicker and more durable. While glaze protects tile from stains, the grout between tiles is still vulnerable because it's so porous. To minimize staining, apply a quality grout sealer, and reapply the sealer once a year thereafter. Choosing larger tiles reduces the number of grout lines. Although the selection is a bit limited, if you choose 13" × 13" floor tile, you can span from the front to the back edge of the countertop with a single seam.

The countertop in this project has a substrate of ¾" exterior-grade plywood that's cut to fit and fastened to the cabinets. The plywood is covered with a layer of plastic (a moisture barrier) and a layer of ½"-thick cementboard. Cementboard is an effective backer for tile because it won't break down if water gets through the tile layer. The tile is adhered to the cementboard with thinset adhesive. The overall thickness of the finished countertop is about 1½". If you want a thicker countertop, you can fasten an additional layer of plywood (of any thickness) beneath the substrate.

Tools & Materials ▶

Tape measure	Ceramic tile
Circular saw	Tile spacers
Power drill	¾" exterior-grade (CDX)
Utility knife	plywood
Straightedge	4-mil polyethylene sheeting
Stapler	Packing tape
Drywall knife	½" cementboard
Framing square	1¼" galvanized deck screws
Notched trowel	Fiberglass mesh tape
Tile cutter	Thinset mortar
Grout float	Grout
Sponge	Silicone caulk
Corner bracket	Silicone grout sealer
Moisture barrier	Cement board screws
Caulk gun	Metal rule

Ceramic or porcelain tile makes a durable countertop that is heat-resistant and relatively easy for a DIYer to create. By using larger tiles, you minimize the grout lines (and the cleaning that goes with them).

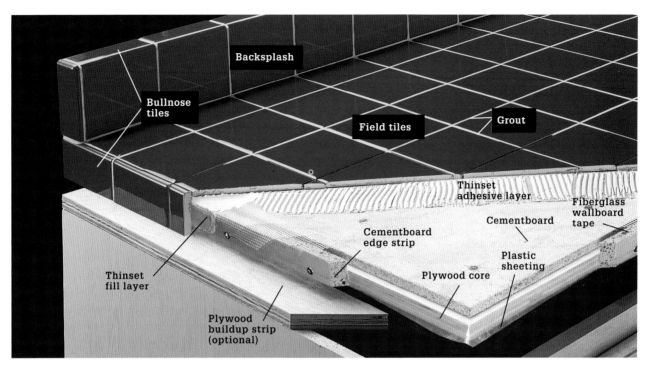

A **ceramic tile** countertop made with wall tile starts with a core of ¾" exterior-grade plywood that's covered with a moisture barrier of 4-mil polyethylene sheeting. Half-inch cementboard is screwed to the plywood, and the edges are capped with cementboard and finished with fiberglass mesh tape and thinset mortar. Tiles for edging and backsplashes may be bullnose or trimmed from the factory edges of field tiles.

Options for Backsplashes & Countertop Edges

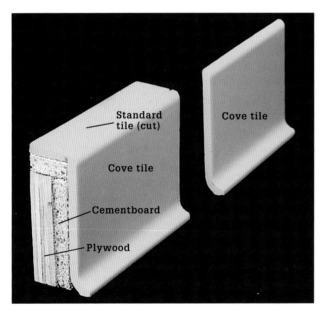

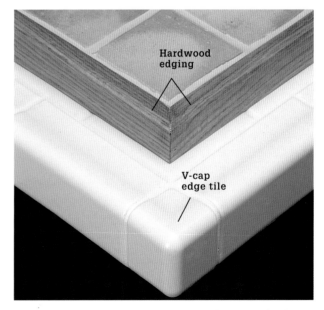

Backsplashes can be made from cove tile attached to the wall at the back of the countertop. You can use the tile alone or build a shelf-type backsplash using the same construction as for the countertop. Attach the plywood backsplash to the plywood core of the countertop. Wrap the front face and all edges of the plywood backsplash with cementboard before laying tile.

Edge options include V-cap edge tile and hardwood strip edging. V-cap tiles have raised and rounded corners that create a ridge around the countertop perimeter—good for containing spills and water. V-cap tiles must be cut with a tile saw. Hardwood strips should be pre-finished with at least three coats of polyurethane finish. Attach the strips to the plywood core so the top of the wood will be flush with the faces of the tiles.

Tips for Laying Out Tile ▶

• You can lay tile over a laminate countertop that's square, level, and structurally sound. Use a belt sander with 60- or 80-grit sandpaper to rough up the surface before setting the tiles. The laminate cannot have a no-drip edge. If you're using a new substrate and need to remove your existing countertop, make sure the base cabinets are level front to back, side to side, and with adjoining cabinets. Unscrew a cabinet from the wall and use shims on the floor or against the wall to level it, if necessary.

• Installing battens along the front edge of the countertop helps ensure the first row of tiles is perfectly straight. For V-cap tiles, fasten a 1 × 2 batten along the reference line using screws. The first row of field tile is placed against this batten. For bullnose tiles, fasten a batten that's the same thickness as the edging tile, plus 1⁄8" for mortar thickness, to the face of the countertop so the top is flush with the top of the counter. The bullnose tiles are aligned with the outside edge of the batten. For wood edge trim, fasten a 1 × 2 batten to the face of the countertop so the top edge is above the top of the counter. The tiles are installed against the batten.

• Before installing any tile, lay out the tiles in a dry run using spacers. If your counter is L-shaped, start at the corner and work outward. Otherwise, start the layout at a sink to ensure equal-sized cuts on both sides of the sink. If necessary, shift your starting point so you don't end up cutting very narrow tile segments.

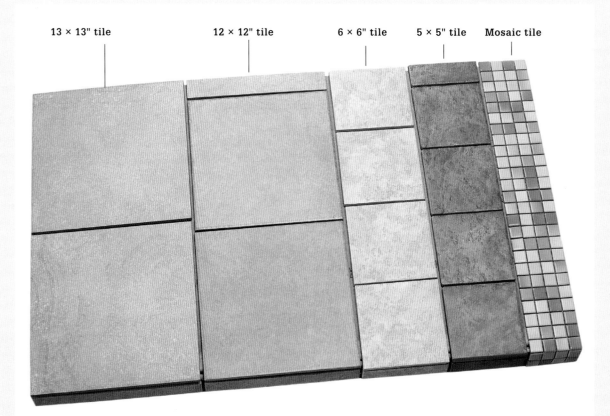

13 × 13" tile   12 × 12" tile   6 × 6" tile   5 × 5" tile   Mosaic tile

The bigger the tile, the fewer the grout lines. If you want a standard 25"-deep countertop, the only way to get there without cutting tiles is to use mosaic strips or 1" tile. With 13 × 13" tile, you need to trim 1" off the back tile but have only one grout line front to back. As you decrease tile size, the number of grout lines increases.

How to Build a Tile Countertop

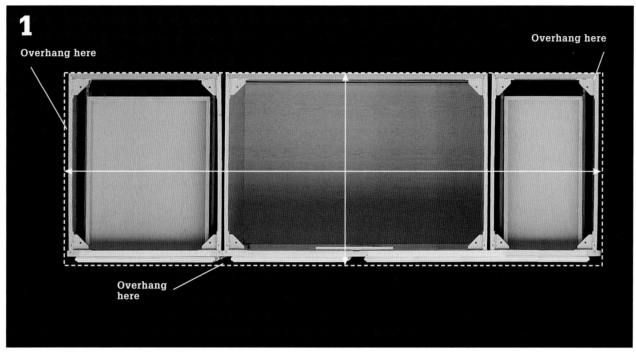

Determine the size of the plywood substrate by measuring across the top of the cabinets. The finished top should overhang the drawer fronts by at least ¼". Be sure to account for the thickness of the cementboard, adhesive, and tile when deciding how large to make the overhang. Cut the substrate to size from ¾" plywood using a circular saw. Also make any cutouts for sinks and other fixtures.

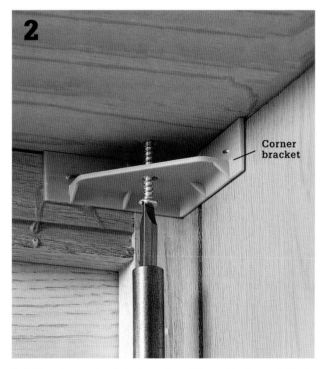

Set the plywood substrate on top of the cabinets, and attach it with screws driven through the cabinet corner brackets. The screws should not be so long that they go through the top of the substrate.

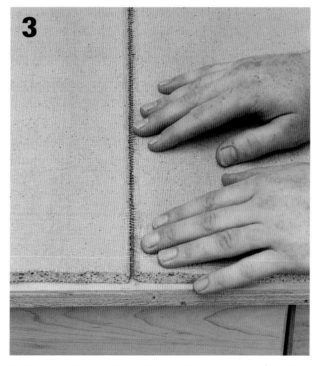

Cut pieces of cementboard to size, then mark and make the cutout for the sink. Dry-fit them on the plywood core with the rough sides of the panels facing up. Leave a ⅛" gap between the cementboard sheets and a ¼" gap along the perimeter.

(continued)

Option: Cut cementboard using a straightedge and utility knife or a cementboard cutter with a carbide tip. Hold the straightedge along the cutting line, and score the board several times with the knife. Bend the piece backward to break it along the scored line. Back-cut to finish.

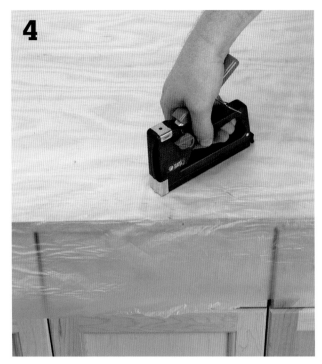

Lay the 4-mil plastic moisture barrier over the plywood substrate, draping it over the edges. Tack it in place with a few staples. Overlap seams in the plastic by 6", and seal them with packing tape.

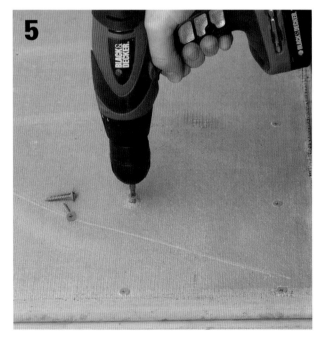

Lay the cementboard pieces rough side up on the plywood and attach them with cementboard screws driven every 6". Drill pilot holes using a masonry bit, and make sure all screw heads are flush with the surface. Wrap the countertop edges with 1¼"-wide cementboard strips, and attach them to the core with cementboard screws.

Tape all cementboard joints with fiberglass mesh tape. Apply three layers of tape along the front edge where the horizontal cementboard sheets meet the cementboard edging.

Fill all the gaps and cover all of the tape with a layer of thinset mortar. Feather out the mortar with a drywall knife to create a smooth, flat surface.

Determine the required width of the edge tiles. Lay a field tile onto the tile base so it overhangs the front edge by ½". Hold a metal rule up to the underside of the tile and measure the distance from it to the bottom of the subbase. The edge tiles should be cut to this width (the gap for the grout line causes the edge tile to extend the subbase that conceals it completely).

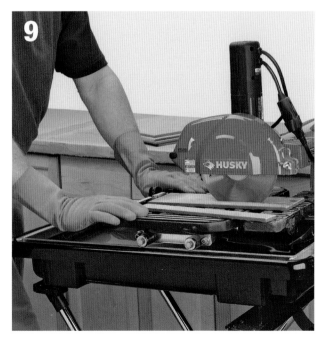

Cut your edge tiles to the determined width using a tile saw. It's worth renting a quality wet saw for tile if you don't own one. Floor tile is thick and difficult to cut with a hand cutter (especially porcelain tiles).

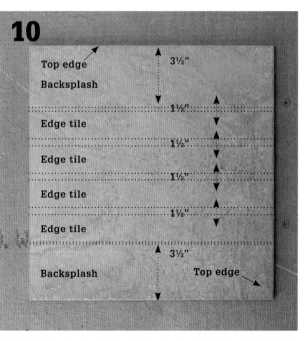

Cut tiles for the backsplash. The backsplash tiles (3½" wide in our project) should be cut with a factory edge on each tile that will be oriented upward when they're installed. You can make efficient use of your tiles by cutting edge tiles from the center area of the tiles you cut to make the backsplash.

(continued)

Sink cutout area

Dry-fit tiles on the countertop to find the layout that works best. Once the layout is established, make marks along the vertical and horizontal rows. Draw reference lines through the marks and use a framing square to make sure the lines are perpendicular.

Variation: Small Floor Tiles & Bullnose Edging ▸

Lay out tiles and spacers in a dry run. Adjust the starting lines, if necessary. If using battens, lay the field tile flush with the battens, then apply the edge tile. Otherwise, install the edging first. If the countertop has an inside corner, start there by installing a ready-made inside corner or by cutting a 45° miter in the edge tile to make your own inside corner.

Place the first row of field tile against the edge tile, separating the tile with spacers. Lay out the remaining rows of tile. Adjust the starting lines if necessary to create a layout using the smallest number of cut tiles.

12

Use a ⅜" square notched trowel to apply a layer of thinset adhesive to the cementboard. Apply enough for two or three tiles, starting at one end. Hold the trowel at roughly a 30° angle and try not to overwork the adhesive or remove too much.

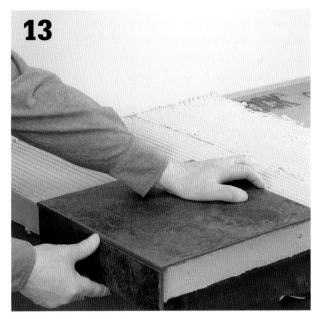

13

Set the first tile into the adhesive. Hold a piece of the edge against the countertop edge as a guide to show you exactly how much the tile should overhang the edge.

14

Cut all the back tiles for the layout to fit (you'll need to remove about 1" of a 13 × 13" tile) before you begin the actual installation. Set the back tiles into the thinset, maintaining the gap for grout lines created by the small spacers cast into the tiles. If your tiles have no spacer nubs, see the option.

Option: To maintain even grout lines, some beginning tilers insert plus-sign-shaped plastic spacers at the joints. This is less likely to be useful with large tiles like those shown here, but it is effective. Many tiles today feature built-in spacing lugs, so the spacers are of no use. Make sure to remove the spacers before the thin set sets. If you leave them in place, they will corrupt your grout lines.

(continued)

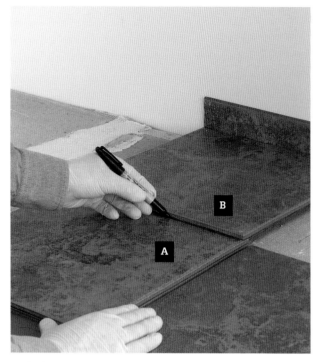

Variation: To mark border tiles for cutting, allow space for the backsplash tiles, grout, and mortar by placing a tile against the back wall. Set another tile (A) on top of the last full tile in the field, then place a third tile (B) over tile (A) and hold it against the upright tile. Mark and cut tile (A) and install it with the cut edge toward the wall. Finish filling in your field tiles.

To create a support ledge for the edge tiles, prop pieces of 2 × 4 underneath the front edge of the substrate overhang using wood scraps to prop the ledge tightly up against the substrate.

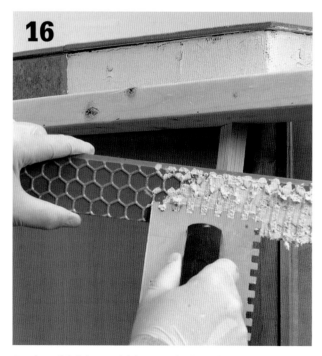

Apply a thick layer of thinset to the backside of the edge tile with your trowel. This is called "buttering" and it is easier and neater than attempting to trowel adhesive onto the countertop edge. Press the tiles into position so they are flush with the leading edges of the field tiles.

Butter each backsplash tile and press it into place, doing your best to keep all of the grout lines aligned.

18

Mix a batch of grout to complement the tile (keeping in mind that darker grout won't look dirty as soon as lighter grout). Press the grout down into the grout line areas with a grout float.

19

Let the grout dry until a light film is created on the countertop surface, then wipe the excess grout off with a sponge and warm, clean water. See the grout manufacturer's instructions on drying tiles and polishing.

20

Run a bead of clear silicone caulk along the joint between the backsplash and the wall. Install your sink and faucet after the grout has dried.

21

Wait at least one week and then seal the grout lines with a penetrating grout sealer. This is important to do. Sealing the tiles themselves is not a good idea unless you are using unglazed tiles (a poor choice for countertops, however).

Granite Tile Countertops

Solid granite countertops are hugely popular today, and for good reason: they are stunningly beautiful, amazingly hard and durable, and completely natural. However, they are also expensive and virtually impossible for a do-it-yourselfer to install. Take heart though, there is a way for an enterprising DIYer to achieve the look and feel of natural granite, but at a fraction of the price: granite tile countertops.

You have two basic product options with granite tile. You can use standard granite tiles, which consist of field tiles and edge tiles with square edges that are installed just like ceramic or porcelain tiles are, and finished with thin edge tiles to create the nosing; or you can use granite tiles that are installed with front tiles that feature an integral bullnose that better imitates the look of solid granite. Typically, granite tiles fit together more snugly than ceramic tiles do. This gives you the option of finishing with grout that's the same color as the tiles for a near-seamless appearance.

Layout is the most important step on any tile project, and no less so when working with granite tiles. If tiles need to be cut to fit, it is best to cut the tiles at the center of the installation or the sets of tiles at both ends. This creates a more uniform look. Granite tile can be installed over laminate countertop (not post-form) if you remove the nosing and backsplash first. The laminate substrate must be in good condition with no peeling or water damage.

Tools & Materials ▸

⅝" exterior-grade plywood	Utility knife
¼" tile backer or cementboard	Straightedge
Cementboard screws	¼" notched trowel
Tiles	Modified thinset
Tile wet saw with diamond blade	Unsanded grout
Honing stone	Grout sealer
Power drill	Stone sealer
Circular saw	Sponge
Jigsaw	Bucket
Compass	Rubber gloves
	Pry bar
	Carpeted mallet

Granite tiles are installed in much the same way as ceramic tiles are, but the ultra-narrow gaps and matching grout mimic the appearance of solid polished granite.

How to Install Granite Tile Countertops

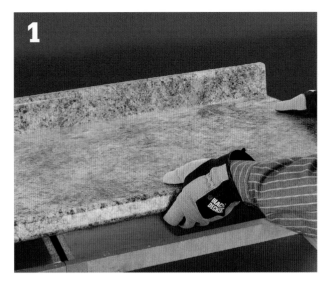

Remove old countertops by unscrewing the countertops from the cabinets. Unscrew the take-up bolts on mitered sections of the countertop. Use a utility knife to cut through any caulk. The countertops should lift off easily; if they don't, use a pry bar to carefully pry them away from the base cabinets. **Note:** In some cases you can install the tiles over old laminate countertops.

Measure the cabinet bank from outside edges to outside edges on all sides and cut a piece of ⅝"-thick exterior-grade plywood to fit. The edges of the plywood should be flush with the outside edges of the cabinet tops. Screw the plywood to the cabinet braces from underneath.

Place the sink upside down in the desired location and trace around it to mark the cutting lines. To create support for the drop-in sink flange, use a compass to trace new cutting lines inside the traced lines (usually ⅝"). See the manufacturer's instructions to confirm dimensions (some sinks come with a template for making the cutout). Use a jigsaw to cut out the sink opening.

Granite tile, like ceramic tile, requires a cementboard or denseboard underlayment layer. Cut the material to the same dimension as the plywood subbase and lay the cementboard over the plywood with the edges flush. From inside the sink base, trace around the sink cutout with a marker. Remove the underlayment and make the cutout with a jigsaw.

(continued)

5

Apply a ⅛"-thick layer of modified thinset to the top of the plywood using a ¼" notched trowel. Screw the cementboard to the plywood with cementboard screws. Space the screws 4" to 5" apart across the entire surface.

6

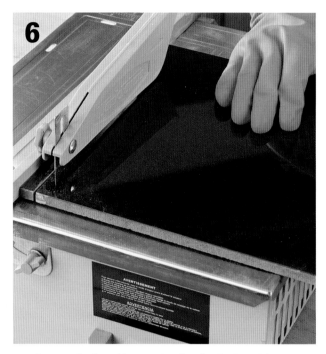

Cut (as needed) and lay out the tiles, beginning with an inside corner if you have one. Arrange tiles for the best color match. Tiles abut directly, with no space for grout. Cut the tiles as necessary to fit. Cut self-edged tiles edge side first. Cut the tiles with the polished side up. Use a fine-honing stone to relieve the cut edge to match the manufactured edges.

Variations for Corners & Angles

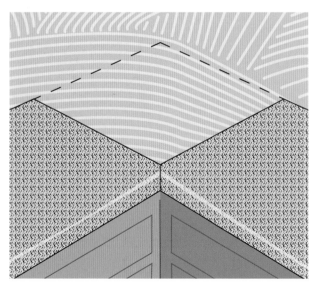

Mitered inside corners are a bit tricky to cut because the mitered point needs to align with the starting point of the bullnose edge. This has the effect of making the corner set back roughly 1 inch.

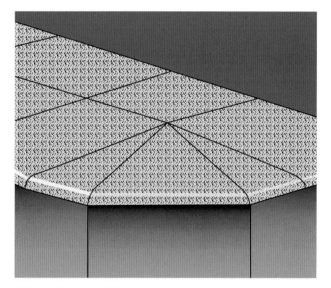

Kitchen islands often have corners that do not form a right angle. In such cases, you can avoid a sharp angle on the countertop by cutting a triangular bullnose piece to fill in.

Even though the flange of the sink shown here will cover the inside corners in the sink cutout, take care to make a gentle rounded corner cut by drilling at the corner with a ½" masonry bit. Perpendicular corner cuts can lead to cracking. Finish the straight legs of the cutout with a tile saw or a jigsaw with a masonry blade.

Start laying tiles. Use modified thinset and a ¼" trowel. If you have an inside corner in your countertop, begin there. Apply thinset at the inside corner, enough to place four or five tiles. Set the left and right inside corner pieces and the first field tile.

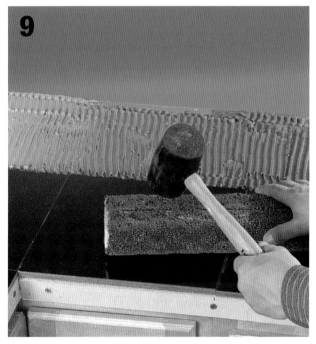

Continue setting tiles. Apply the thinset mortar to an area big enough for two to four tiles and place the tiles. Use a 2 × 4 covered with carpeting to set the tiles. Push down on tiles to set, and also across the edges to ensure an even face.

After the thin set has dried for at least 24 hours, grout with an unsanded grout. When the grout has dried, seal with natural stone sealer.

Tile Backsplash

There are few spaces in your home with as much potential for creativity and visual impact as the space between a countertop and wall-mounted cabinets. A well-designed backsplash can transform the ordinary into the extraordinary. Tiles for the backsplash can be attached directly to wallboard or plaster and do not require backerboard. When purchasing the tile, order 10 percent extra to cover breakage and cutting. Remove the switch and receptacle coverplates, and install box extenders to make up for the extra thickness of the tile. Protect the countertop from scratches by covering it with a drop cloth.

Tools & Materials ▸

Level
Tape measure
Pencil
Tile cutter
Rod saw
Notched trowel
Rubber grout float
Beating block
Rubber mallet
Sponge

Bucket
Story stick
Straight 1 × 2
Wall tile
Tile spacers (if needed)
Mastic adhesive
Masking tape
Caulk
Drop cloth
Grout

Tip ▸

Break tiles into fragments and make a mosaic backsplash. Always use a sanded grout for joints wider than ⅛".

Contemporary glass mosaic sheets create a counter-to-cabinet backsplash for a waterproof, splash-proof wall with very high visual impact.

How to Install a Tile Backsplash

Make a story stick by marking a board at least half as long as the backsplash area to match the tile spacing.

Starting at the midpoint of the installation area, use the story stick to make layout marks along the wall. If an end piece is too small (less than half a tile), adjust the midpoint to give you larger, more attractive end pieces. Use a level to mark this point with a vertical reference line.

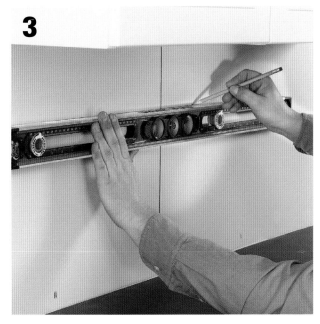

Although it may appear straight, your countertop may not be level and therefore is not a reliable reference line. Run a level along the counter to find the lowest point on the countertop. Mark a point two tiles up from the low point and extend a level line across the entire work area.

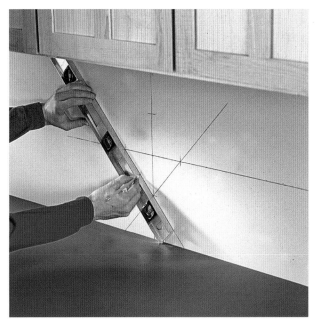

Variation: Diagonal Layout. Mark vertical and horizontal reference lines, making sure the angle is 90°. To establish diagonal layout lines, measure out equal distances from the cross point, and then connect the points with a line. Additional layout lines can be extended from these as needed.

(continued)

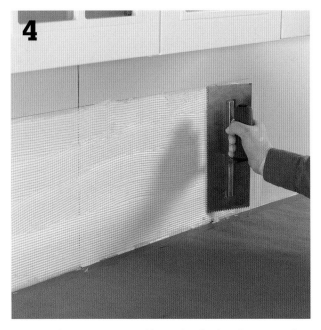

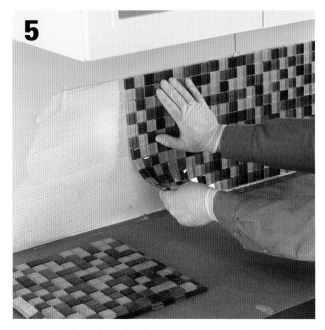

Protect the countertop with a strip of painter's tape. Apply mastic adhesive evenly to the area beneath the horizontal reference line using a notched trowel. Comb the adhesive horizontally with the notched edge.

Press tiles into the adhesive with a slight twisting motion. If the tiles are not self-spacing, use plastic spacers to maintain even grout lines. If the tiles do not hang in place, use masking tape to hold them in place until the adhesive sets.

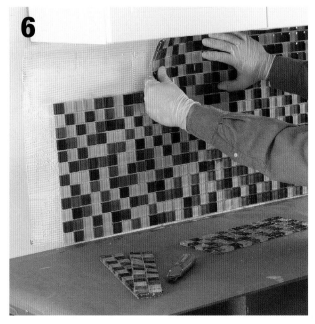

Install a whole row along the reference line, checking occasionally to make sure the tiles are level. Continue installing tiles below the first row, trimming tiles that butt against the countertop as needed.

Install an edge border as needed or desired. Mosaic sheets normally do not have bullnose tiles on the edges, so if you don't wish to see the cut edges of the outer tiles, install a vertical column of edge tiles at the end of the backsplash area.

8

When the tiles are in place, make sure they are flat and firmly embedded by laying a beating block against the tile and rapping it lightly with a mallet. Remove the spacers. Allow the mastic to dry for at least 24 hours, or as directed by the manufacturer.

9

Mix the grout and apply it with a rubber grout float. Spread it over the tiles, keeping the float at a low 30° angle, pressing the grout deep into the joints. **Note:** For grout joints ⅛" and smaller, be sure to use a nonsanded grout.

10

Wipe off excess grout, holding the float at a right angle to the tile, working diagonally so as not to remove grout from the joints. Clean any remaining grout from the tiles with a damp sponge, working in a circular motion. Rinse the sponge thoroughly and often.

11

Clean excess grout with a damp sponge. When the grout has dried to a haze, buff the tile clean with a soft cloth. Apply a bead of caulk between the countertop and the tiles.

Installing a recycled paper countertop requires moderate DIY skills and attention to detail. But the result, as seen here, is a stunning surface that is both unique and lasting. This particular product is a full 1½" thick. Thinner versions are available and may be easier to fabricate.

Recycled Paper Countertops

If you're on the hunt for a handsome, distinctive, durable, and eco-friendly countertop, you're not likely to do better than a recycled paper surface. Countertops like the PaperStone® product used in this project are 100 percent post-consumer recycled paper, emitting no volatile organic compounds (VOCs) and certified "food safe" by the National Safety Foundation (NSF).

You might not think that paper would make for effective countertop surface—especially in water-prone rooms such as kitchens and bathrooms. But fortunately, you'd be wrong. This material is non-porous and stain resistant. It can withstand heat up to 350°F (although many finishes used to seal the surface cannot), and scratches can be buffed or sanded out.

There are a few restrictions with this type of countertop. You should never use a bleach cleanser, and although cuts can be buffed out, it's best to use a cutting board rather than cutting directly on the countertop. You should also be aware that the counter comes in different thicknesses—we've used the thickest version here to show the fabrication and installation steps more clearly; a thinner panel (with a built-up edge) would be easier for the home DIYer to work with.

Tools & Materials ▸

- Circular saw with fine-tooth carbide blade
- Biscuit joiner
- Router with carbide bits
- Hole saw (1³⁄₈")
- Jigsaw
- Take-up bolts
- Measuring tape
- Cordless power drill with an assortment of drill bits
- Carpenter's level
- Caulk gun
- Painter's tape
- 2-part epoxy
- Silicone adhesive
- Silicone caulk
- Orbital sander with an assortment of grits (80 to 240)
- Maroon nonwoven pads
- Straight edge and radius guides
- Recycled paper countertop panels
- Sink/stove templates (included with sink/stove or available online)
- Speed square
- Bar clamps
- Acetone

This PaperStone countertop product is a full 1½" thick. It can be cut with normal cutting tools, but give yourself plenty of time.

How to Install a Recycled Paper Countertop

1

Check that the cabinets are secure and level. Measure twice and make a precise drawing of the entire countertop surface, including the location of seams, to optimize the surface area of the panels you order. Note the exact sink, faucet, and stove opening center points.

2

Fabricate the template for the countertop using cardboard. Set the cardboard on top of the base cabinets and trace the outline on the underside. Note overhangs, appropriate anchor screw locations, and other features. Scribe the template to the wall on the backside (the fit can be less accurate if you are installing a backsplash). **Note:** Plan for joining countertop sections, using butt seams rather than miter seams.

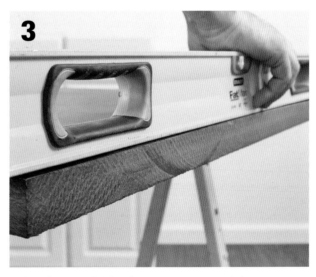

3

Order the panel(s) for the countertop. Recycled paper counters have a "grain" and slight variations across the surface; decide the best panel orientation when you have it in the space. Inspect the panel(s) to determine if there is a crown, which should face up. Check manufacturer's directions, however, because some recommend flattening any crown prior to installation.

4

Position the template over the panel and clamp it in place. Trace the template outline on the panel top face, and mark the position of fixtures such as sinks. We used a silver marker on this product, which can be removed later with acetone.

Remove the cardboard and position any sink, faucet, and fixture templates on the panel. Trace outlines for fixtures, checking the number and diameter of faucet holes (normally 1" diameter). Recheck all measurements against the master drawing, before cutting the panel.

Cut the material to length using a circular saw equipped with an 80- to 100-tooth, triple-chip carbide blade. Cut approximately 1/8" outside of the marked line. Also use the circular saw to make straight portions of the sink cutout (for the sink, cut 1/8" inside the cutting line).

Use a jigsaw and fine-tooth carbide blade to make curved cuts (be sure that the blade is kept perpendicular to the countertop's surface during cutting). Drill faucet holes with a hole saw. Use a router with a guide to make clean-up cuts precisely to the traced line. Use a radius guide with the router on inside radius corners.

Use an random orbit sander to smooth out the cuts, sanding up to the cutting line as needed. For long edges, you can speed things up by using a belt sander to remove material. Finish-sand all edges with180- to 220-grit sandpaper.

Test-fit the countertop(s) in position on the cabinet bases and check for appropriate and correct alignment. Specifically, check that all cutouts are in the correct positions, that any overhangs are consistent, and that the surface is level across its span.

Rout exposed countertop edges to the preferred profile, using the appropriate router bit and a guide. Move the router steadily along the edge and avoid sitting too long at any one spot, which can lead to burn marks. (continued)

11

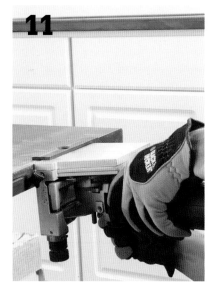

Dry-fit the countertop sections to ensure a tight fit. To help with alignment, mark and cut matching biscuit slots in the edge of each countertop, using a biscuit joiner.

12

Turn the countertops over and mark T channels for the take-up bolts. Note that the channels must be exactly mirrored on the connecting countertop. Check that the marks line up when the countertops are correctly aligned. Rout the channels using a plunge router set to a depth half of the panel's thickness. Set the biscuits in the slots, coat the countertop seam edges with the adhesive recommended by the manufacturer (normally a two-part epoxy), and secure the countertops tightly with bar clamps. Install the take-up bolts, check once again that the seam is precisely aligned—in particular, that no portion of the top seam surface is higher than any other—and tighten the bolts.

13

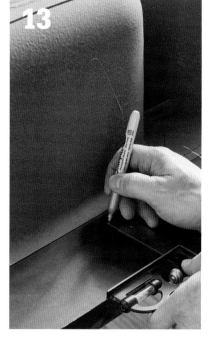

Install an undermount sink before installing the counter. (Drop-in sinks are installed after.) Mark the edges of the sink and the edges of the sink cutout with centerline marks. With the countertop upside down, align the sink over the opening mark for the mounting screw guide holes.

14

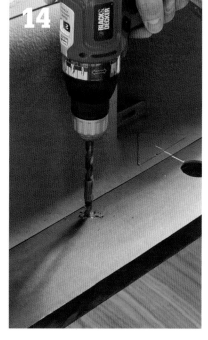

Drill guide holes for the sleeves that will hold the sink-mounting clips. Insert the sleeves into the holes.

15

Apply a bead of silicone caulk to the sink flange. Set the sink into position in the underside of the countertop. Install the sink clips to secure the sink in place.

Remove all clamps. With several helpers, carefully invert the countertop so it is rightside-up. Apply beads of silicone caulk to the tops of the cabinets and then lower the countertop in place.

Locate the anchor screw locations on the cabinet top frames and drill pilot holes using a carbide bit and a drill stop. Secure the countertop in place with screws driven into the pilot holes. Tap the sink if needed to adjust its position, and then finish tightening the mounting screws.

Wipe away any squeeze out or excess adhesive from around the sink and underside edges of the counter as well as along any seams. Use a clean cloth dipped in acetone to clean up the adhesives.

Measure, mark, and cut the backsplash sections from the leftover panel segments. (Sections should be joined with 90° butt seams.) Test-fit the backsplash sections in place. (Although they can be scribed to the back wall profile, this is usually unnecessary because the caulk will fill any gap.) Add a profile to the top of the backsplash as desired, using a router and bit.

Lay a thin bead of silicone adhesive on the back and bottom of the backsplash sections. Carefully press the backsplash pieces into place and wipe away any squeezeout or excess adhesive. Allow the adhesive to cure according to the manufacturer's directions.

(continued)

21

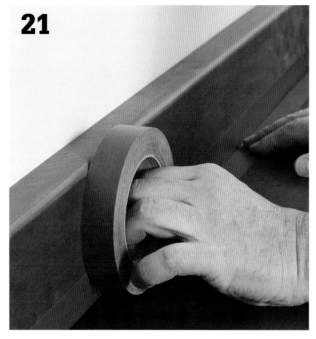

Clean all exposed surfaces using a clean, wet cloth, and let dry. Use painter's tape or masking tape to mark of the backsplash for caulk along both the countertop seam and the wall seam. This will ensure crisp caulk lines. Apply a thin bead of caulk along the seams.

22

Remove the tape and allow the caulk to cure entirely. Use a general-purpose woven hand pad to rub down the entire countertop surface. Use 180- to 240-grit sandpaper to smooth any rough edges or profiles.

23

If you want a perfectly smooth finish, sand the top and edges beginning with a 180-grit pad and working up to a 240-grit pad. Clean the surface between sandings, using a clean, lint-free cloth moistened with denatured alcohol. **Note:** Check the manufacturer's recommendations—many types of recycled paper countertops have a textured surface that will not support a smooth finish.

24

Apply a sealer to the countertop surface for a rich color. If the manufacturer does not sell a product made for their counters, like the PaperStone sealer seen here, you can use food-safe mineral oil in most cases. Buff the surface for a nice sheen.

Resources

Aristokraft Cabinetry
www.aristokraft.com

Cambria Natural Quartz Countertops
www.cambria.com

Dupont Corian
www2.dupont.com

EcoTop Surfaces
www.kliptech.com

Formica Surfaces
www.formica.com

Granite Transformations
www.granitetransformations.com

IKEA Home Furnishings
www.ikea.com

KraftMaid Kitchen and Bathroom Cabinets
www.kraftmaid.com

Merillat Cabinets
www.merillat.com

National Kitchen & Bath Association
800-843-6522
www.nkba.org

PaperStone Sustainable Composite Surfaces
www.paperstoneproducts.com

Pyrolave
www.pyrolave.com

Silestone Quartz Surfaces
www.silestoneusa.com

Vetrazzo
www.vetrazzo.com

Wilsonart
www.wilsonart.com

Photo Credits

Photos courtesy of Cambria, www.cambriausa.com:
pp. 9 (top both), 167 (right)

Todd Caverly, pp. 106

Photos courtesy of Dupont/Corian®, www2.dupont.com,
800-441-7515: pp. 11 (lower), 163 (left), 149 (top)

Photos courtesy of Formica Corporation,
www.formica.com, 800-367-6422: page 8 (top and
lower right)

Photos courtesy of Granite Transformations,
www.granitetransformations.com: pp. 11 (top left),
163 (right)

Photos ©IKEA®, www.ikea.com: pp. 13 (lower), 49, 50,
51 (top left and lower two)

iStock: pp. 11 (top right), 70, 72, 81, 164

Photo courtesy of KlipTech®, www.kliptech.com:
pp. 12 (top right)

Photo courtesy of Kohler Plumbing, www.kohler.com,
pp. 51 (top right)

Photos courtesy of Kraftmaid®, www.kraftmaid.com:
pp. 6, 14 (top right), 29 (all), 40, 59

Photos courtesy of Merillat®, www.merillat.com:
pp. 13 (top left), 14 (lower left), 88

Photos courtesy of PanelTech/PaperStone®,
www.paperstoneproducts.com, 360-538-9815: pp. 12
(top left and lower), 165 (lower), 166 (left)

Photos courtesy of Pyrolave, www.pyrolave.fr: pp. 9
(lower, both)

Eric Roth for Thomas Buckborough: pp. 172

Photo courtesy of Shutterstock.com/©Artazum:
pp. 39 (both)

Photo courtesy of Shutterstock.com/©Lipskiy: pp. 28

Photo courtesy of Shutterstock.com/©MarishaSha:
pp. 48

Photos courtesy of Vetrazzo, www.vetrazzo.com: pp.
10 (all), 162, 167 (left)

Photo courtesy of Wilsonart LLC, www.wilsonart.com:
pp. 8 (lower left)

Conversions

Metric Equivalent

Inches (in.)	1/64	1/32	1/25	1/16	1/8	1/4	3/8	2/5	1/2	5/8	3/4	7/8	1	2	3	4	5	6	7	8	9	10	11	12	36	39.4
Feet (ft.)																								1	3	3 1/12
Yards (yd.)																									1	1 1/12
Millimeters (mm)	0.40	0.79	1	1.59	3.18	6.35	9.53	10	12.7	15.9	19.1	22.2	25.4	50.8	76.2	101.6	127	152	178	203	229	254	279	305	914	1,000
Centimeters (cm)							0.95	1	1.27	1.59	1.91	2.22	2.54	5.08	7.62	10.16	12.7	15.2	17.8	20.3	22.9	25.4	27.9	30.5	91.4	100
Meters (m)																								.30	.91	1.00

Converting Measurements

TO CONVERT:	TO:	MULTIPLY BY:
Inches	Millimeters	25.4
Inches	Centimeters	2.54
Feet	Meters	0.305
Yards	Meters	0.914
Miles	Kilometers	1.609
Square inches	Square centimeters	6.45
Square feet	Square meters	0.093
Square yards	Square meters	0.836
Cubic inches	Cubic centimeters	16.4
Cubic feet	Cubic meters	0.0283
Cubic yards	Cubic meters	0.765
Pints (U.S.)	Liters	0.473 (Imp. 0.568)
Quarts (U.S.)	Liters	0.946 (Imp. 1.136)
Gallons (U.S.)	Liters	3.785 (Imp. 4.546)
Ounces	Grams	28.4
Pounds	Kilograms	0.454
Tons	Metric tons	0.907

TO CONVERT:	TO:	MULTIPLY BY:
Millimeters	Inches	0.039
Centimeters	Inches	0.394
Meters	Feet	3.28
Meters	Yards	1.09
Kilometers	Miles	0.621
Square centimeters	Square inches	0.155
Square meters	Square feet	10.8
Square meters	Square yards	1.2
Cubic centimeters	Cubic inches	0.061
Cubic meters	Cubic feet	35.3
Cubic meters	Cubic yards	1.31
Liters	Pints (U.S.)	2.114 (Imp. 1.76)
Liters	Quarts (U.S.)	1.057 (Imp. 0.88)
Liters	Gallons (U.S.)	0.264 (Imp. 0.22)
Grams	Ounces	0.035
Kilograms	Pounds	2.2
Metric tons	Tons	1.1

Converting Temperatures

Convert degrees Fahrenheit (F) to degrees Celsius (C) by following this simple formula: Subtract 32 from the Fahrenheit temperature reading. Then mulitply that number by 5/9. For example, 77°F - 32 = 45. 45 × 5/9 = 25°C.

To convert degrees Celsius to degrees Fahrenheit, multiply the Celsius temperature reading by 9/5, then add 32. For example, 25°C × 9/5 = 45. 45 + 32 = 77°F.

Fahrenheit   **Celsius**

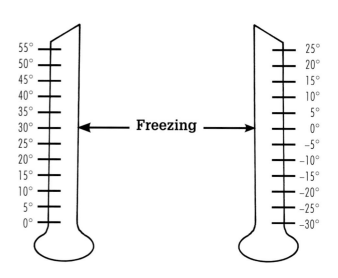

Index

(continued)

Also available in this Series

Where Homeowners Go for Expert Answers

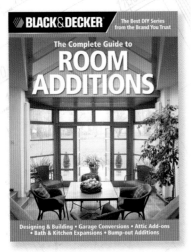

ISBN 978-1-58923-482-6

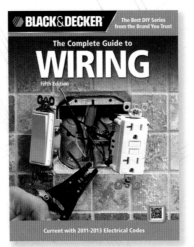

ISBN 978-1-58923-601-1

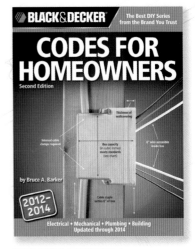

ISBN 978-1-58923-721-6

Complete Guide to Bathrooms

Complete Guide to a Better Lawn

Complete Guide to Built Ins

Complete Guide to Carpentry for Homeowners

Complete Guide to Ceramic Tile

Codes for Homeowners

Complete Guide to Decks

Complete Guide to Finishing Basements

Complete Guide to Flooring

Complete Guide to Garages

Complete Guide to Garden Walls & Fences

Complete Guide to Gazebos & Arbors

Complete Guide to a Green Home

Complete Guide to Greenhouses & Garden Projects

Complete Guide to Kitchens

Complete Guide to Landscape Projects

Complete Guide to Masonry & Stonework

Complete Guide to Outdoor Carpentry

Complete Guide to Patios & Walkways

Complete Guide to Plumbing

Complete Guide to Roofing & Siding

Complete Guide to Room Additions

Complete Guide to Sheds

Complete Guide to Windows & Entryways

Complete Guide to Wiring

Complete Outdoor Builder

Complete Photo Guide to Home Repair

Complete Photo Guide to Home Improvement

Complete Photo Guide to Sheds, Barns & Outbuildings

Advanced Home Wiring

Trim & Finish Carpentry

Working With Drywall

To view other titles
in the *Black &
Decker Complete
Guide* book series
scan this code

COOL
SPRINGS
PRESS
Home and Garden Experts™

400 First Avenue North • Suite 400 • Minneapolis, MN 55401 • www.creativepub.com